Organization
The Effect on Large Corporations

Research in Business Economics and Public Policy, No. 2

Fred Bateman, Series Editor

Chairman and Professor
Business Economics & Public Policy
Indiana University

Other Titles in This Series

Organization
The Effect on Large Corporations

by
Barry C. Harris

UMI RESEARCH PRESS
Ann Arbor, Michigan

658.402
H 313

Produced and distributed by
UMI Research Press
an imprint of
University Microfilms International
Ann Arbor, Michigan 48106

Library of Congress Cataloging in Publication Data

Harris, Barry C. (Barry Clifford)
Organization, the effect on large corporations.

(Studies in business economics ; no. 2)
"A revision of the author's thesis, University of
Pennsylvania–Economics, 1979"–T.p. verso.
Bibliography: p.
Includes index.
1. Industrial organization–United States. 2. Executives
–Salaries, pensions, etc.–United States. 3. Corporate
profits–United States. 4. Corporations–United States.
I. Title. II. Series.

HD70.U5H37 1983   658.4'02   83-3589
ISBN 0-8357-1435-7

To my parents

Contents

Tables

1

The Multidivision Hypothesis: Historical and Theoretical Bases

The American industrial enterprise has shown a remarkable ability to adjust to changes in its environment. Numerous studies have been made of the reactions of businesses to changes in technology, population, and governmental policy. These studies have been historical, theoretical, and statistical in nature. One of the adaptive responses available is the form in which firms organize themselves. Economic literature contains many studies which discuss the separation of management from ownership in the modern corporation. The tendency for a corporation in which management is separated from ownership to not behave in a profit maximizing manner has received a great deal of attention. Like most economic studies of firm performance, these studies have usually failed to include the firm's organization as a factor which explains managerial behavior. If organization form does affect the firm's performance, this is a serious omission.

As large corporations grew and diversified they often experienced efficiency losses which resulted from the increased complexity associated with the growth and diversity. The problems which these firms experienced and the manner in which the firms dealt with these problems are detailed in a book written by Alfred D. Chandler, Jr.[1] Chandler identified the formation of a multidivisional organization as the key adaptive response used by corporations in correcting the inefficiencies caused by increased diversification. Later work by Oliver E. Williamson[2] examined the multidivisional organization and compared its ability to maintain efficient behavior in the diversified corporation to that of a functional form organization. Williamson's work is drawn largely from the literature on organization theory. He concluded that the multidivisional form of organization is superior to the functional form in organizing complex diversified tasks. More formally he proposed the multidivision form hypothesis, which states:

> the organization and operation of the large enterprise along the lines of the M-form [multidivisional form] favors goal-pursuit and least-cost behavior more nearly associated

with the neo-classical profit-maximization hypothesis than does the U-form [functional form] organizational alternative.[3]

One goal of the analysis that follows is to test the multidivision form hypothesis statistically. A second purpose is to examined statistically the ways in which the firm's behavior under a multidivisional form is different than under a functional form. The statistical work is discussed in chapters 2 and 3. Chapter 2 examines the effect of organization form on the level of a particular expenditure of the firm—executive compensation. In chapter 3 the multidivision form hypothesis is tested directly. The effect of the firm's adoption of the multidivisional form on its profitability is examined. Several case studies are presented in chapter 4. Conclusions are discussed in chapter 5.

The remainder of this chapter is in three parts. The first part explains the system used to categorize the organization forms used by the firms. The second part reviews the adaptive responses used by firms in response to changes in their environment. Most of this work is based on the Chandler study. The third part discusses the theoretical underpinnings of the multidivision form hypothesis.

A Method for Categorizing Organization Forms in Large Firms[4]

If the performance characteristics of the M-form organization are to be compared with those of the U-form firm, a systematic evaluation of the organizational history of the firms in the sample needs to be undertaken. This requires that a methodology be developed which distinguishes organization forms.

The M-form organization involves more than simple divisionalization. Without the proper internal control and auditing devices, the divisionalized firm's executive office is not able to perform properly the allocation of resources among divisions. Thus a simple dichotomy between functionally organized firms and those which have divisionalized will assign firms to the M-form category which are not of the type contemplated by the multidivision hypothesis.

Firms included in the samples which were used to perform the statistical tests reported in chapters 2, 3, and 4 were assigned organization forms according to the following method. These samples included only those firms for which an accurate organizational history could be constructed.

U-Form

The U-form firm is the type which has been described as having a centrally controlled functional organization. In the U-form organization, the functional departments are given day-to-day operating responsibility. These departments operate in such areas as sales, manufacturing, and engineering. The top executive of each of these departments is usually a member of the executive office. The executive office, while having the responsibility for long-term strategic decision making, also coordinates and evaluates the activities of the functional departments. The executive office has both operational and strategic responsibilities. Often a U-form firm will include one or more subsidiaries which operate independently from the rest of the firm. When controls of the M-form type are lacking, U-form firms with subsidiaries are designated to have a U-H form organization.

M-Form

The M-form firm is one in which operating authority is assigned to divisions organized along either product or geographic lines. The divisions are designated as profit centers. That is, divisions are expected to maximize their profits. The executive office has the responsibility for strategic decision making. In carrying out this responsibility, the executive office audits and evaluates the performance of the divisions and allocates capital among the divisions based on the relative performances of the divisions.

H-form

The H-form firm is divisionalized like the M-form firm. The H-form firm, however, lacks the auditing and control devices present in the M-form firm. Examples of this organization type can be found among the conglomerates, such as LTV, which formed in the 1960s.

M'-Form

The M'-form organization is the transitional form of the M-form organization. This typically means that the M-form structure is in place, but some element is not performing in a way consistent with the M-form definition.

$\overline{M}$-Form

The $\overline{M}$-form firm is one which has been divisionalized, but in which members of the executive office are involved in day-to-day operating decisions.

X-Form

The X-form firm is similar to the U-H form firm. The major part of the X-form firm is centralized and organized along functional lines. In addition, the X-form firm includes subsidiaries which have the same control relationship to the major part of the firm as an M-form division has to the executive office. The executive staff of the large functional division serves as the staff of the whole firm.

Organization Form in the Industrial Enterprise: A Historical Perspective

Chandler's hypothesis is that a firm's strategy, which he defines as its plan for the allocation of resources to meet anticipated demand, determines its structure. Structure is defined as an enterprise's design for integrating its existing resources to meet current demand. Long-term decisions made by a firm set into motion forces which later make it necessary for the firm to adapt its organization to the changing situation. That is:

> Unless new structures are developed to meet new administrative needs which result from an expansion of a firm's activities into new areas, functions, or product lines, the technological, financial and personal economies of growth, and size cannot be realized.[5]

The Adoption of the Centralized-Administrative Functional Organization

Chandler observes that the pattern of firms first developing strategies in an attempt to meet changing market conditions and then developing a structure to rationalize the results of its strategy has occurred twice in modern American business history. The first of these cycles began after the Civil War. Rapid industrialization and urbanization combined with an improving transportation system gave firms the opportunity to meet growing and newly developed demands. Industrial enterprises got larger. Some expanded by acquiring plant, equipment, and personnel. Others were created from the consolidation of several smaller producers. Typically, expansion was followed by the firm integrating vertically, both forward and backward, in an effort to obtain assured markets and sources of raw materials.

Resource accumulation of this type occurred in most industries between 1880 and World War I. As a result, the firm faced both new problems and opportunities. Instead of being solely a manufacturing entity, the newly expanded firm now had a distribution network and raw material sources to administer. Raw material supply needed to be coordinated with production, as did the firm's marketing efforts. The response of most firms was to adopt a centralized, functionally organized structure.

This structure resulted from the desire of the firm to reduce the cost of production. Functional activities needed to be organized such that waste and redundancy were minimized. Because each firm was engaged in a few closely related activities it was possible to place each functional activity, such as production or sales, in its own department. Each department had the day-to-day responsibility of carrying out its assigned function. Within each department lines of authority and communication were established. Each department had the job of coordinating, appraising, and evaluating its functional activity.

The coordination of the functional activities of the departments was the responsibility of the central office. Firms in some industries experienced problems in coordinating the functional departments. These problems were greatest in industries which either manufactured for the final consumer or made a product with exact and changing specifications. The inability to anticipate demand more than a short time into the future often caused inventory problems. If the sales department sold goods which were not being produced, customers would be lost. If the production department produced goods which were not being sold, inventory would accumulate.

The problem of coordinating the activities of the sales and manufacturing departments was most critical in industries producing consumer durables. Consumer durable production was usually characterized by high levels of investment, a large number of steps in production, complex functional units, a production process which was difficult to adjust and for which the failure to adjust properly was costly, and costs which were sensitive to changes in demand.

These characteristics made it necessary to be able to adjust to short-run changes in demand. The centralized administrative functional organization provided the method. The functional departments had the responsibilities of coordination, appraisal, and planning within each department. The central office had the responsibilities of coordinating the activities of the functional departments with the firm's perceptions of the market, both present and expected. As Chandler notes:

> Whether planned or not, the new central office eventually developed three types of duties. One critical role became the coordination and integration of the output of the several functional departments to changing market demands, needs, and tastes. This included the coordination of product flow from one functional department to another, an activity whose development is strikingly illustrated in the Jersey Standard case. It also required the maintenance of cooperation between the manufacturing, sales, and development of engineering departments regarding the improvement or redesign of products. Second, expansion and vertical integration encouraged the growth of auxiliary or service departments in the central office which could relieve the administrative load on the functional departments by taking over more specialized activities. Finally, besides coordination activities with the market and providing specialized services, the central office, of course, allocated the future use as well as appraised the present performance of the resources of the enterprise.[6]

Both the jobs of coordinating and integrating the outputs of the functional departments and of allocating resources for future use and evaluating their present use required that the central office possess accurate data. While in some corporations it took a long time to occur, eventually, a department was created which had the responsibility of gathering and evaluating data. This data usually included market data as well as internal cost data. Though some information was collected and transmitted by a corporate-wide department, most information was still collected by the functional departments. Chandler notes that:

> In department building, the development of statistics and other information to flow through the lines of communication proves less a challenge than it did in setting up of the administrative offices at the next two levels.[7]

Because the activities undertaken and the language spoken by field people and by people on the corporate staff when performing a specific function were similar, common accounting and reporting systems naturally evolved.

The corporate financial department, which handled routine financial transactions within the departments as well as the company's external financial transactions, was often the department which was given the assignment of providing information for planning, coordinating, and evaluating the work of the other departments. In a sense the financial department became the bridge between the day-to-day activities of the departments and the long-term activities of the central office.

Eventually, formal budgets and methods of appropriation systematized the long-term allocation of resources. This meant that the executives in the central office needed to make fewer basic entrepreneurial decisions and could now concentrate on strategic decisions. The collection of data and its evaluation allowed the strategic decisions to be based on both short-run and long-run expectations of demand for the market in which the firm operated.

The Adoption of the Multidivisional Organization

As long as the firm concentrated its efforts in one relatively homogenous activity, the centralized functional form was a natural and efficient way for the firm to organize its activities. The responsibilities of the functional departments were easily specified and their performance easily evaluated. The central office's coordination of the functional departments and strategic planning was based on data which was easy to interpret since it concerned closely related goods. However, several factors made it likely that firms would look for new markets. These factors included declining profitability in existing markets, the development of new technology, and the shifting of population into new geographic areas.

The search for new markets developed along both geographic and product lines. Expansion into new product lines was usually based on the products which the firm already manufactured and sold. New products, even those based on existing products, were often sold to a new set of customers. The new customers often had different needs than the customers of the older product, thus necessitating new marketing methods. This was the experience of DuPont during the 1910s and early 1920s. In general, firms which experienced the greatest diversification were those firms which were based on a range of technological expertise rather than those firms which made specific end products. Firms with a range of technological expertise were better situated to enter into new product areas which were perceived to be profitable.

As firms diversified, new activities were integrated into the existing functional organization. As long as the new activities were similar to the traditional activities of the firm, their integration into the old organization was not too difficult. However, when the new activities involved either different production techniques or a new set of customers the strain on the organization often became great.

Each line of business had its own functional activities. Because the nature of a particular functional activity in one line of business often differed from the nature of the same functional activity in another line of business, it became increasingly difficult to coordinate the activities of the functional departments and to place responsibility for their performance. As a result performance suffered. When performance suffered, the firm's top executives became more involved in the day-to-day activities of the functional departments.

> Executives responsible for over-all planning, coordination and appraisal became increasingly enmeshed in operational activities. They had neither the time, the information, nor the inclination necessary to stick to entrepreneurial and strategic decision making. The details of the departmental activities for which they were responsible had priority over what seemed vague long-term planning and appraisal. Moreover, each was a specialist rather than a generalist.... Worse yet, just because each such senior officer viewed the company's problems from the point of view of a single function, he tended to reflect, in appraising, planning, and coordinating the activities of the enterprise as a whole, the outlook of one of the parts.[8]

The heads of the functional departments increasingly abdicated their firm-wide outlook in favor of one of advocacy for the parochial views of their departments.

> To make matters worse, objective data on departmental performance proved hard to devise, if only because profit and loss in one activity depended so much on the work accomplished in another. Moreover, the information on which both appraisal and planning had to be based came largely from the departments involved. Administrative decisions often evolved from the give and take of biased individuals using biased data.[9]

When the firm was engaged in only one major activity its top executives were able to handle both the operational and the tactical problems of the firm. Many of the decisions had become routinized. When needed, information which was largely unbiased could be obtained. All the executives were engaged in the one business and knew, to a large degree, what to expect from the functional departments. The amount of room for local maximizing behavior within the functional departments was minimized. In the more complex expanded firm these opportunities increased, necessitating a greater involvement by the top executives.

> The inherent weakness in the centralized, functionally departmentalized operating company and in the loosely held, decentralized holding company became critical only when the administrative load on the senior executive officers increased to such an extent that they were unable to handle their entrepreneurial responsibilities efficiently. This situation arose when the operations of the enterprise became too complex and the problems of coordinating, appraisal, and policy formation too intricate for a small number of top officers to handle both long-run, entrepreneurial and short-run, operational administrative activities.[10]

The adaptive response to these problems was the multidivisional organization. The key element of the new organization was that it separated strategic decisions from operating decisions. The firm's top executive staff was given the responsibility of making long-term strategic decisions. Operating divisions were created to carry out day-to-day decisions. The divisions typically were organized as small firms in one clearly defined line of business. The stated objective of each division usually was to maximize its profits.

Because they operated in clearly defined product areas, the problems which had developed in the diversified functionally organized corporation were not likely to occur in the divisionalized firms's divisions. Hence the divisions were usually organized along functional lines. This allowed the divisions to take advantage of the natural economies which resulted from the functional form. Procurement of inputs, production techniques, sales, and even such areas as research and development were responsibilities of the divisions.

Having been freed from the need to allocate a large amount of their time to operational details, the general staff was free to concentrate on long-term problems such as planning, evaluation of the divisions' performance, and allocation of resources. Planning could now take the broader tactic of identifying markets which the firm viewed as being profitable. The evaluation of a division's performance was less complex than had been the evaluation of functional departments. Divisions were engaged in a clearly defined market and were profit centers. This meant that their performance could be summarized by one statistic. It was possible to compare the profitability of a division with that of other firms in the market and other divisions within the firm. By contrast, it was difficult to evaluate the work done by a functional department without engaging in great detail. Each department's performance depended to a large degree on that of other departments. In addition, the perceived goals of the departments could be in conflict with each other.[11] The lack of a common measure of performance from department to department had also been troublesome.

In many ways the allocation of resources in the multidivision firm was an extension of the evaluation of the divisions' performances. The divisions, being quasi-firms, were in competition for the scarce resources of the firm. The firm's top staff allocated the firm's resources to those divisions which it felt would produce the highest profits.[12] Often this meant that a greater share of resources was given to those divisions which historically had been the most profitable. By contrast, it is impossible to "reward" in this way departments in the functionally organized firm which demonstrate superior performance. Because the operations of the functional departments are so interrelated, it usually does not make sense to expand the operations of one functional department without also expanding the operations of others.

The flow of unbiased information was imperative for the general staff of the divisionalized firm to perform its job properly. Unlike the functional organization, where data was primarily collected and transmitted by the functional units, the collection and transmission of data in the multidivisional organization was primarily the responsibility of the financial department. This department was part of the elite group which was responsible to the general staff. Besides providing the general staff with more and higher quality data, the information flow from the financial department gave the general staff an independent means by which requests, proposals, and estimates from the divisions could be checked.

The properly defined multidivisional organization thus was composed of several divisions. These divisions each operated in a clearly defined market. The divisions had the day-to-day operating responsibilities for their respective markets. The divisions were expected to maximize their profits. The firm's general office concerned itself with the longterm health of the firm and did not become entangled in the operational affairs of the divisions.[13] These long-term concerns included the allocation of resources among the divisions and the evaluation of the performances of these divisions. The general office performed *ex ante* and *ex post* evaluations of the allocation of resources. Each division attempted to maximize its profits in competing for the firm's scarce resources. If the general office allocated the firm's scarce resources to the divisions according to their expected profitability, then the firm's profits were maximized. In this way the corporate staff became a capital market internal to the firm.

Organizational Form in the Industrial Enterprise: A Theoretical Perspective

In the previous section, the problems encountered by centralized functionally organized firms as they expanded and diversified were discussed. The functional organization, which was seen to be an effective organization for firms operating in one well-defined market, was not able to handle the increased decision-making complexity many firms encountered as they expanded into additional markets. The purpose of this section is to examine the causes of these problems. Much of this discussion is drawn from Oliver Williamson's paper "Managerial Discretion, Organization Form, and the Multi-Division Hypothesis."[14] Williamson sees the firm's performance being affected primarily in two ways as the result of its expansion and continued use of the centralized functional organization. The first way is the efficiency loss within the firm due to what he calls cumulative control loss. The second way results from the manner in which strategic decisions are made.

The Effects of Expansion on the Functionally Organized Firm

Cumulative Control Loss. As the functionally organized firm expanded, each of its functional departments had responsibilities in different and sometimes diverse industries. The activities of these departments needed to be coordinated and evaluated by the general office. What had been a relatively straightforward duty in the simple firm became a complex and difficult task in the expanded firm. The specification of goals for each of the functional departments became difficult. As an example, not only did the production department have to be told to minimize its costs, but a diverse product mix needed to be specified. Problems of this type might not have been too troublesome if the decision had been made only in the production department. However, the production mix was strongly influenced by the activities of the sales department. In addition, production required inputs which were often purchased by a third functional department. When the various functional departments set their own schedules based on their own forecasts, as was sometimes the case, the results were often rather chaotic.

Because the work of each functional department is so dependent upon the work of the others, the cost to the firm of either poor performance by one department or poor coordination between the departments can be rather high. As a result it became imperative that the firm attempt a more comprehensive coordination of the activities of the functional departments. Additional coordination, however, required additional levels of hierarchy. The addition of hierarchial levels may result in loss of control by the top executives. Williamson explains:

Finite spans of control naturally require additional hierarchial levels to be introduced as the U-form [functionally organized] enterprise expands. Adding hierarchial levels can, if only for serial reproduction reasons, lead to an effective loss of control through incomplete or inaccurate transmittal of data moving up and instructions moving down the organizational hierarchy. . . . data are summarized and interpreted as they move forward and instructions are operationalized as they move down. If, however, the functional units of the firm view the hierarchial structure as affording opportunities to pursue local goals, deliberate distortions may be introduced into the hierarchial exchange process.[15]

Even if the people working in the functional departments do not desire the maximization of local goals over the goals of the firm the increased levels of hierarchy will still tend to result in some control loss. The information flows between the functional units and the central staff are still subject to distortion. Information needs to be edited. Complete information is seldom communicated from one hierarchial level to another. Editing can cause a distortion of the information if the various levels have different goals, have access to different facts, or have different perceptions of the facts on which their action is premised.[16]

Because information is incomplete and sometimes wrong, even a profit-maximizing member of a functional unit would not necessarily make decisions which contribute to the firm's profits.

An apparently simple way to allocate the function of decision-making would be to assign to each member of the organization those decisions for which he possesses the relevant information. The basic difficulty in this is that not all the information relevant to a particular decision is possessed by a single individual.[17]

This is the problem referred to previously in which the interconnectedness of the functional departments' activities compounded the difficulties caused by the inability to specify goals in the functional departments. Because information is not communicated easily among the functional departments, the options are either to set up decoupling devices which reduce the amount of information the decision-making units need or to set up lines of communication which lead to one person. The former, without a change in organization, is subject to quickly diminishing returns. The latter is subject to control loss. These problems were observed by Bernard:

Under most ordinary conditions, even with simple purposes, not many men can see what each is doing or the whole situation, nor can many communicate essential information regarding or governing specific action without a central channel or leader. But a leader likewise is limited in time (and capacity) in communicating with many persons contemporaneously, . . . [18]

Alterations in the Strategic Decision Process. Besides cumulative control loss, the expanding functionally organized firm can experience problems due to changes in its strategic decision-making process. If the problems of cumulative control loss are dealt with by assigning a greater amount of operating responsibility to the chief executive officer, a "Gresham's Law of Organization" is experienced. Day-to-day operational problems need to be addressed. Because the capacity of the office of the chief executive is limited, the increased concentration on operational problems tends to place strategic decisions into the background.

In functionally organized firms, the office of the chief executive has often used the heads of the functional departments to expand the executive office's capacity to make strategic decisions. A natural result, however, is for the heads of the functional departments to represent their departments in strategic decision making instead of representing the firm. Williamson describes this process:

> Expansion also eventually overcomes the capacity of the office to provide strategic planning and maintain effective control. The usual means for augmenting this capacity has been to bring the heads of the functional divisions into the peak coordination process. The natural posture for these functional executives to take is one of advocacy in representing the interests of their respective operating units.[19]

If the advocacy stance of the various functional department heads balanced each other, this problem would not be too great. However, these advocacy stances tend to produce biases towards more services which can only be accommodated by increasing expansion by the firm. As the firm expands an increasingly permissive attitude towards organizational slack develops. It is easy to see why this occurs. Since the various members of the executive staff, including the heads of the functional departments, only have imprecise knowledge of each functional department's production function, it is difficult for them to ascertain each department's needs and to evaluate its performance. That is, in the complex firm it is difficult to distinguish between the real needs of the functional departments and those needs which the department's advocate presents as being real. A certain amount of bargaining may eliminate some of the nonessential desires of the departments, however it is doubtful that all can be eliminated. Since each department head has the best knowledge of that department's production function, each department head is in a position to demand more resources for the department. Without this knowledge other members of the executive staff are reluctant to eliminate too much of the department's requests.

The development of an expansionary bias and a permissive attitude towards slack is a result of the inability to distinguish between proper and improper requests from the functional departments. A growing firm offers opportunities to satisfy, in the short run, the non-profit-maximizing requests of the functional departments. As a result there is a permissive attitude towards slack. Slack allows each department to provide a buffer between itself and other departments. This is helpful to the department in achieving its goals. If it were easy to evaluate each department's performance, slack would not be desired by the departments. In the complex functionally organized firm, however, departmental evaluations can be difficult. The firm as a whole has some desire to provide a buffer for the departments, but the problem can become critical as the room for discretionary behavior in the operating units increases and thus so does their desire for slack.

The Capital Market as a Constraint on Inefficient Behavior

The capital market is usually viewed as the control device which corrects a firm's tendencies away from the profit-maximizing ideal. The idea being that as a firm moves away from profit-maximizing behavior its profitability falls. As profitability falls so does the price of the firm's equity. A falling stock price, *ceteris paribus,* makes the firm more desirable as an acquisition. Because a takeover is usually not desired by existing management, the capital market has been viewed as a good efficiency control device.

This reasoning is correct in the absence of transaction costs. The capital market, however, is not a perfect and costless method of assuring efficiency. It is an external device which may have high transaction costs associated with its use. Being an external control device, the capital market operates without having access to a host of information which is readily available internal to the firm. The capital market reviews summary statistics, such as profitability, which may be subject to short-run aberrations due to random or extraordinary events which have no effect on the firm's long-term performance. The firm may be able to distinguish between reduced profitability due to poor management and that due to random or extraordinary events. Yet it is possible that the firm is unable to transmit this information to the capital market at an acceptable cost.

Even in those instances where the capital market has access to sufficient information to make the correct determination with regard to a firm's decline in profitability, there still are reasons why the capital market may not perform satisfactorily as an efficiency control device. For one, the capital market is not designed as a fine-tuning device. Either a takeover is initiated or it is not initiated. In addition, the cost of using the capital market is quite high. A takeover bid disrupts the business environment and imposes costs whether it is successful or unsuccessful. A great deal of management's energies are devoted to the takeover proceedings. In addition, the existing management may initiate defensive behavior which is not in the long-term interest of the firm. The discrete manner in which the capital market polices efficiency, coupled with the high cost of using it, makes the capital market an inappropriate device for controlling efficient behavior except in relatively unusual situations. Williamson has summarized these ideas:

> In a general sense the most severe limitation the capital market encounters is that it is an external control device. . . . The displacement threat which the capital market poses is subject to nontrivial displacement costs if the incumbent management is disposed to resist the takeover effort. . . . Not only are the original costs of securing displacement apt to be significant, but once displacement is accomplished the successful takeover agency needs to face the transition costs which a displacement involves.[20]

The Multidivisional (M-Form) Organization

The inability of the capital market to react to the inefficiencies of the increasingly complex functionally organized firm provided management with an opportunity to make the appropriate changes necessary to arrest increasing inefficiencies. The organizational innovation adopted by many managements was the multidivisional (M-form) organization. The main idea of the M-form organization is to separate the executives who make strategic decisions from day-to-day operating decision making. This is done by assigning operating responsibilities to divisions or "quasi-firms" which are organized either along product or geographic lines. The firm's general office is assigned the function of evaluating the performance of the divisions, allocating resources among the divisions, and making the firm's long-term strategic decisions.

The divisions are typically designed as scaled down functionally organized firms. Because each division has responsibility in a limited area it is not subject to the same degree of control loss as the more complex functionally organized firm. The M-form division is generally given the responsibility to maximize profits. That is, the M-form division is a profit center.[21]

The firm's executive office and its staff have the broader commitment to the overall firm. The executive office, besides having departments such as the financial and legal departments which are more centralized by their nature, also has departments such as manufacturing, sales, and purchasing. Unlike their counterparts in the functionally organized firm, these latter departments have no operational responsibilities, but rather have advisory and auditing responsibilities. It is the advising and auditing functions of the executive office which give the M-form organization the ability to serve as an effective internal capital market and efficiency control device. Without the ability to audit and advise the divisions, the M-form general staff would not have the information necessary to allocate effectively capital in accordance with the firm's overall goals. These goals are advanced through the executive office's concern with strategic decisions including those involving planning, appraisal, and control. Included among these is the allocation of resources among the operating divisions.

Diagram of a Typical M-form Organization

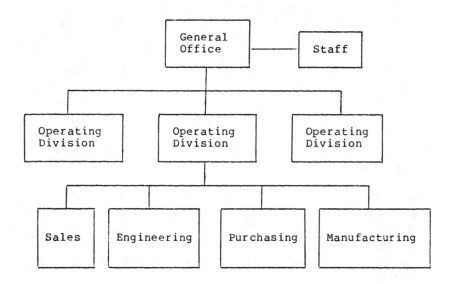

Strategic Decision Making Within the M-Form Firm. The executive office needs to be given the time, incentives, and capacity to deal with strategic decisions. Strategic decision making is improved in the M-form firm compared to its U-form counterpart by separating the executive office from the operating divisions. This gives the people in the executive office the time they need. Incentives are also improved by separating the executive staff from the operating units. By giving them responsibility for the overall firm, members of the executive staff are less likely to assume an advocacy role. In addition, the opportunities for non-profit-maximizing behavior by staff members are reduced due to the relatively small size of the staff. The needed capacity is supplied by augmenting the executive office with a staff. It is important that this staff be kept small. Otherwise problems such as over-documentation and staff expansion biases may occur.

In many ways it is its staff which allows the executive office to perform the duties of coordination and control necessary in an M-form firm. The staff performs such services as conducting both *ex ante* market studies and *ex post* evaluations of the divisions' performance and supplying data to the executive office. The data supplied by the staff are an independent check on those provided by the divisions. The divisions have the easiest access to data which are pertinent to its operations. The divisions also have incentives to distort to their advantage information which flows to the executive office. The staff's *ex ante* market studies and *ex post* evaluations provide the executive office with additional independent checks. Because they deal with the day-to-day operations, the divisions have access to information about changes in the market, new opportunities, the performance of competitors, and the underlying causes of their performance. For example, new opportunities for the firm may not be reported by a division if the opportunity would require that a new division be established. An existing division may view a new division as being a competitor for scarce corporate funds. A second example already discussed is the need to distinguish divisional performance based on either random or extraordinary events and that based on more underlying long-term considerations. Divisions wish to make poor performance appear to be the result of either random or extraordinary events, and may distort information to this end. Distortion in information provided by the divisions is lessened by the independent checks provided by the staff's market studies, evaluations, and supply of data.

Internal Control Within the M-Form Firm. Internal control is highly interconnected with strategic decision making in the M-form firm. Internal control requires that resource allocation be rationally related to performance. The auditing, evaluation, and data supply functions provided by the executive office staff give the firm's top executives the ability to relate resource allocation to performance.

M-form divisions are usually established as independent profit centers. As a result a division's performance can be measured in an unambiguous manner. This is difficult to do with functional units within a U-form firm since the performance of each functional unit depends on that of the other functional units. In addition, because the M-form divisions are separable, resources can be allocated to those divisions which have performed best or have new opportunities. Because of the executive staff's access to internal firm data, it is better able to allocate resources to its divisions than could the capital market.

> Internal resource allocation can be regarded both as a market substitute and an internal control technique.... *Ceteris paribus,* those parts of the organization that are realizing superior performance will increase in relative size and importances, ... [22]

Because the most profitable divisions are "rewarded" with increased resources, divisions have the incentive to maximize profits. In this way the goals of the divisions are made more consistent with those of the firm. It is possible for the executive office to provide an array of incentives to managers of divisions which further increase the compatability between the goals of the firm and the divisions.

Non-Profit-Maximizing Opportunities in the M-Form Firm. The Multidivision Hypothesis is stated in comparative institutional terms. No claim is made that the M-form organization is immune from discretionary behavior by its employees. The Multidivision Hypothesis says that a complex diversified firm will behave more like a neoclassical profit-maximizing firm when organized as M-form than when organized as U-form. In this section some of the problems which can occur in an M-form firm are discussed.

1.   The Size of Divisions and Complexity. M-form divisions are organized as profit centers. They are essentially simple quasi-firms organized as U-form. The U-form organization is desirable as long as the division does not become too complex. If the division does become too complex, it is subject to the same types of problems as other U-form organizations.

2.   Non-Separability of Divisions. In some cases some M-form divisions cannot be separated from each other. The vertically integrated firm with a monopoly supply division has been discussed. In the case of the monopoly supply division the proper assignment of transfer prices is critical. If the price is set too low, a greater than firm-wide profit-maximizing output will be produced. If the price is too high, output will be too low.

3.   Long-run vs. Short-run Profit Maximization. The M-form divisions may substitute short-run profit maximization for long-run profit maximization, which is the firm's goal. Because the division's production function is not precisely known by the executive staff, the division does have some ability to behave in a discretionary manner. An example which is often discussed in the planning literature is that of risk. Managers are reluctant to take on risky projects that consume a great deal of resources even if the expected profitability of the project makes it warranted. This is particularly likely to occur when the project is not expected to produce profits for a fairly long period. The firm may be able to share the risk, but it is unlikely that the division is also able to do so. Because of the asymmetry of information, the division may successfully avoid the project. A continuing substitution of short-term for long-term profit maximization should become known to the executive office. However, if the pattern does not become apparent to the executive office until after a significantly long period, the division's former manager may be in a new position, possibly enjoying the fruits of the short-term profit maximization. Also, with new divisional management in place it may be difficult to judge if the lower performance is the result of the first manager's decisions or their execution by the second manager.

4.   Divisional Advocacy. A division's managers may assume an advocacy stance with the executive office. They may wish to have funds allocated to their division past the level which maximizes firm profits. This results from a desire to see the division grow in size and importance. By a judicious use of incentives and resource allocation the executive office should be able to keep this potential problem small.

5.   Executive Office Staff Size. The staff assigned to the executive office may be too small or too large. If the staff is too small, it will be unable to provide the services discussed above. If this results, the divisions will be more able to behave in a discretionary manner. The holding company form (H-form) discussed above is an example. If the staff is too large, it may be prone to many of the problems associated with the U-form result. The staff may become too involved in day-to-day decisions. A tendency to over-document may result.

2

Executive Compensation

In this chapter the effect of organization form on executive compensation is investigated. Previous studies of executive compensation have neglected to consider the effects of organizational form. These studies have instead concentrated on sales and profits as the prime determinants of executive compensation. The reason that these studies have used this approach can be traced to a 1932 study by Adolf A. Berle and Gardiner C. Means.[1] Berle and Means asserted that management had become separated from ownership. This separation, coupled with an increasing diffusion of ownership, made it more probable that management would pursue goals other than stockholder welfare maximization. In previous analyses sales and profits have been investigated to see to what extent the utility maximization of top executives is tied to the economic interest of stockholders through the executives' compensation package. This study looks at the question in a slightly different way. Executive compensation is viewed as a potential form of discretionary behavior. Again, the hypothesis that the large M-form (divisionalized) corporation controls the opportunistic exercise of discretion better than the comparable U-form (centralized) corporation is examined.

Background: Theory

Neoclassical

If executive compensation is determined according to the usual neoclassical standards, its level will be a function of the "amount" (quality) of managerial talent necessary to maximize stockholder welfare. Yarrow has constructed such a model.[2] In this model profits are maximized with respect to [X_n], the n-vector of factors of production, and Q, the quality of executive management. He obtains the following first order conditions:

$$\frac{\partial \pi}{\partial X_i} = 0 \qquad (i = 1, 2, \ldots, n)$$

$$\frac{\partial \pi}{\partial Q} = s'(Q)$$

where s(Q) is the cost function for the executive input and π is the profit of the firm before the deduction of executive compensation. Since every firm faces the same s(Q), the quality and compensation of executives are determined by those factors that determine the executive's marginal revenue product. In the model it is suggested that capital, labor, and staff may be possible factors that are complementary to executive input. In general, the quantities of these inputs all increase as the size of the firm increases. The neoclassical theory then gives support to a positive link between executive compensation and sales.

If the quantity of all inputs (X_i) is the same for two firms and the two firms pay different levels of compensation to their executives, the neoclassical theory predicts that there exist levels of profit at least as high in the firm with the higher compensation as in the firm with the lower compensation.[3] Similarly, if the quantity of all inputs (X_i) is the same for two firms and one firm is making a higher level of profit, the firm with the higher profit level is expected to pay its executives a higher level of compensation. If executive mobility is not completely free and the executive is not able to capture his full marginal revenue product, the neoclassical theory also gives support to a positive link between executive compensation and profits.

Managerial

Managerial models of the firm view management as hired professionals. The manager, not being an owner, maximizes a utility function that includes arguments other than profit. "Managerial discretion models of the business firm are intended to apply to firms where competitive conditions are not typically severe and where the management may therefore enjoy significant discretion in developing its strategy."[4]

William Baumol characterizes the manager as being a sales maximizer, subject to a constraint on the minimum level of profits. Baumol partially supports this characterization with the observation that "executive salaries appear to be far more closely correlated with the scale of operations of the firm than its profitability."[5]

A model formulated by Oliver Williamson has a managerial utility function that includes preferences for staff, managerial emoluments ("discretionary additions to salary"), and discretionary profit ("the algebraic difference between reported [after tax] profit and minimum profit demanded").[6] Williamson's model predicts that some of the profit of the firm will be absorbed as emoluments. The exact amount depends on the tax rate on firm profits.

Organizational

Herbert Simon has proposed a theory of compensation for the chief executive based on the number of levels in the organization's bureaucracy.[7] Simon asserts (with some casual empirical evidence) that a differential will exist between the salary of an executive and that of his immediate subordinates not only in absolute terms but also as a ratio (i.e. an executive will have a salary b times that of his immediate subordinates). If salaries at the bottom of the hierarchy are determined in a competitive market (as Simon feels is the case)[8] and the levels of hierarchy are considered set at a point in time, then the salary of the chief executive is determinant. Specifically, Simon formulates the relationship as:

$$\text{Log } C = \frac{\log b}{\log n} \log S + \text{constant}$$

where:

C $=$ compensation of the chief executive

b $=$ ratio of each executive's salary to the salary of his immediate subordinates

n $=$ number of immediate subordinates to each executive

S $=$ number of executives in the organization

This equation results from Simon's assertions about organizational structure and its relationship to compensation. If each executive has approximately n subordinates and there are L levels of hierarchy, the number of executives in the organization (S) equals $1 + n + n^2 + \ldots + n^L - 1/n-1$ which is approximately equal to $n^L/n-1$. Taking logarithms this becomes Log S = L log n + constant. If each executive has a salary b times the salaries of the immediate subordinates and if executive entry level salaries equal A, then the salary of the top executive (C) will equal Ab^{L-1} or Bb^L. Taking logarithms this becomes Log C = L log b + constant. Eliminating L from both logarithmic equations yields Simon's equation:

$$\text{Log } C = \left(\frac{\text{Log } b}{\text{Log } n}\right) \text{Log } S + \text{constant}$$

This theory concludes that an inverse relationship between the size of immediate staff and executive compensation exists, after the effects of firm size have been considered.

The second organizational model presented is that which the central thesis of this study is concerned. If executives are viewed as having positive expense preferences, as suggested by Williamson,[9] the multi-firm hypothesis predicts that the organizational form of the firm should affect the level of executive compensation. To the extent that executive compensation can be viewed as being open to discretionary behavior by management, compensation of the top executives should be lower in the M-form firm than in the U-form firm, after the other determinants of compensation are accounted for.

Background: Statistical Studies

David R. Roberts (1959)[10]

Roberts looks at a cross section sample of 410 corporations for the years 1945, 1948, and 1949, plus 939 corporations for 1950. His definition of compensation includes salary plus bonus, which for the periods studied made up the bulk of executive compensation. Roberts found that after airlines and utilities were removed from his sample, industry differences failed to explain differences in compensation. Roberts uses partial correlation analysis to examine the effects of firm size and firm profitability on executive compensation. Because of the high correlation (.911) between the size variable (sales) and the profitability variable (dollar profits), his results are inconclusive. When he looks at only those firms with a low correlation between size and profitability, he finds a much higher correlation between compensation and sales than between compensation and profits. Partial correlation analysis is repeated using rate of return on sales (profits/sales) as the profitability measure. Sales alone accounts for 39% of the variation of compensation. Sales plus rate of return accounts for 42% of the variation.

McGuire, Chiu, and Elbing (1962)[11]

McGuire, Chiu, and Elbing use a cross section sample of 45 of the 100 largest American corporations for each year from 1953 through 1959. Their definition of compensation includes salary plus bonus. Like Roberts, they look at net correlations between compensation and sales and compensation and profits. Using various lag structures, they find a highly significant relationship between compensation and sales. They fail to find a similarly significant relation between compensation and profits. Like Roberts's work, this type of analysis fails to identity the direction of causation. Because of the lag structure employed, McGuire, Chiu, and Elbing conclude that causation runs from sales to compensation.

Lewellen and Huntsman (1970)[12]

Lewellen and Huntsman use cross-section data at three-year intervals from 1942 to 1963. Their analysis uses multiple regression techniques. The basic relationship they postulate is:

$$C_{it} / A_{it} = a_0(1/A_{it}) + a_1(\pi_{it}/A_{it}) + a_2(S_{it}/A_{it})$$

where:

C_{it} = compensation of the chief executive

π_{it} = firm profits

S_{it} = firm sales

A_{it} = firm net assets

Two definitions of C_{it} are used. The first definition includes salary plus bonus. The second definition adds to the first deferred remuneration, retirement income, and stock options. The division by A_{it} and the suppression of the constant term were done to correct for heteroscedasticity. The authors find the coefficients of the profit term to be positive and significant in each year when compensation includes only salary and bonus. The coefficients of the sales term fail to be significant in any year. The more inclusive definition of compensation gives results slightly inferior to those of the less inclusive definition. Lewellen and Huntsman attribute this occurrence to short-term fluctuations which affect the value of stock options in the more inclusive compensation term. The exercise is repeated with the market value of common stock substituted for profits without any significant changes in the results. Lewellen and Huntsman feel the difference between their results and those of Roberts and McGuire, Chiu, and Elbing can be attributed to the more complete multivariate model they employed.

Yarrow (1972)[13]

Yarrow employs a cross section sample of 85 large U.S. industries for the years 1963, 1965, and 1968. He uses a definition of compensation that includes salary, bonus, and deferred income (not adjusted for present values). Stock options are not included. Yarrow looks at several equations of the form:

$$\log (\text{E.C.}) = C_0 + C_1 X + C_2 \text{Sell} + C_3 \pi$$

where:

E.C.	=	executive compensation
X	=	a scale variable. Yarrow ran separate regressions for sales, total assets, capital, and number of employees.
Sell	=	selling and administrative expense
π	=	rate of return on capital

In each of the three years for which the regression is run capital and total assets are the first and second most significant scale variables, with significance levels above .99. In general the scale variables are significant. In every case, the coefficient for the scale variable has a positive sign. With the exception of the regression which uses sales as the scale variable with 1963 data, selling and administrative expense has a significant coefficient. The sign of all these coefficients is positive. In no case is the coefficient for the rate of return variable significant. When the same relationships are examined, with industry differences taken into account by dummy variables, capital remains the strongest scale variable. The coefficient is strongly significant with a positive sign. Both selling and administrative expense and rate of return have coefficients that turn out to be insignificant. In his conclusions, Yarrow points out that the lack of a significant relationship between compensation and profitability may be the result of a specification error. He feels differences in profitability may only be a reflection of industry differences and not of the marginal productivity of the manager. When industry differences are taken into account by looking at different regressions, Yarrow feels a significant relationship between compensation and profitability will emerge.

Masson (1971)[14]

Masson uses a sample of 39 firms in the electronics, aerospace, and chemical industries. The sample for each firm covers the years 1947-66. Masson uses an inclusive definition of compensation, similar to that employed by Lewellen.[15] This definition includes salary, bonus, deferred income, retirement benefits, and stock options. The estimating equation is of the form:

$$(\% \Delta \text{E.C.})_t = b_0 + b_1 \% \Delta S_t + b_2 \% \Delta S_{t-1} + b_3 \% \Delta \text{EPS}_t + b_4 \% \Delta \text{EPS}_{t-1} + b_5 \% \Delta \text{NW}_t + b_6 \% \Delta \text{NW}_{t-1}$$

where:

$(\%\Delta E.C.)$ = percentage change of executive compensation in year t

$(\%\Delta S)_t$ = percentage change in firm sales in year t

$(\%\Delta EPS)_t$ = percentage change in earnings per share in year t

$(\%\Delta NW)_t$ = percentage change in rate of return on a share of stock for year t

This regression is estimated in time series for each firm. The estimated coefficients are then compared cross-section. Masson desribes the statistical technique: "The statistical aggregation technique used is the 'zero test' which assesses the degree of confidence the investigator may have that a random sample of positive and negative numbers are not drawn from a distribution with equal probability of positive and negative numbers."[16] Among the hypothesis tested are:

1) $b^5 + b^6 > 0$ compensation is positively related to increasing value of stock
confidence level: 0.999

2) $b^1 + b^2 < 0$ compensation is negatively related to sales.
confidence level: 0.63

3) $b^3 + b^4 \leq 0$ profits have a negative relationship with compensation, independent of the net worth effect.
confidence level: 0.84

Masson also examines the hypothesis that the form of the compensation package effects the performance of the firm. He finds that the form of the compensation package does effect the performance of the firm. A firm that stresses the return on stock in its compensation package will have its stock perform better than those firms that do not.

Statistical Analysis

The analysis that follows is drawn from a pooled sample of nineteen firms in the food industry for the years 1952-72. The nineteen firms[17] all are among the 250 largest American corporations, by sales, as listed in the June 1972 *Fortune 500*. One industry is chosen in an attempt to minimize heterogeneity among the firms in the sample. Admittedly, the firms form a far from homogeneous sample. The food industry is chosen because the firms in the sample exhibit a high variance of organizational form, both in cross-section and over time within individual firms.

Compensation data for the chief executive officer in each of the companies in the sample was collected. The title of the chief executive officer varies from company to company. For most of the companies in the sample, the position of chief executive officer carries the title of President, with the title of Chairman of the Board connoting a somewhat honorary position. Various definitions of executive compensation are used.[18] The simplest definition includes only current remuneration plus bonuses. The second definition adds deferred remuneration and retirement benefits. The third definition also adds the value of stock options. As explained in appendix A, two different definitions of the value of stock options are used. One definition assumes that all stock options not exercised by December 31, 1973, are not exercised. The second definition assumes that all stock options not exercised by December 31, 1973, are exercised on December 31, 1973, if the option price is less than the December 31, 1973, market price. All compensation is evaluated at its after-tax value.

The two relationships that are being investigated are of the form:

2-1: $\log(EC)_{it} = b_0 + \sum_{i=1}^{19} D_i\, b_{1i} \log(Sales)_{it-i} + \sum_{i=1}^{19} D_i\, b_{2i} \log(profitability)_{it-1}$

$$+ b_3 U_{it} + b_4 M_{it} + b_5 Years$$

and

2-2: $\log(EC)_{it} = c_0 + \sum_{i=1}^{19} D_i\, c_{1i} \log(Sales)_{it-i} + \sum_{i=1}^{19} D_i\, c_{2i} \log(profitability)_{it-1}$

$$+ \sum_{i=1}^{19} D_i\, c_{3i} \log\left(\frac{Sell\ x}{Sales}\right)_{it-1} + c_4 U_{it} + c_5 M_{it} + c_6 Years$$

where:

$$EC_{it} = \text{Executive compensation of firm i at time t, divided by the consumer price index.}$$

$$Sales_{it-1} = \text{Sales of firm i at time t-1.}$$

$$Profitability_{it-1} = \text{Net (after tax) profitability of firm i at time t-1.}$$

$(\text{Sell } X/\text{Sales})_{it-1}$ = Selling and administrative expense, divided by sales of firm i at time t-1.

D_i = Firm dummy. $D_i = 1$ if firm i; $D_i = 0$ otherwise.

U_{it} = Organization dummy. $U_{it} = 1$ if firm i has a U-form organization at time t; $U_{it} = 0$ otherwise.

M_{it} = Organization dummy. $D_{it} = 1$ if firm i has an M-form organization at time t; $M_{it} = 0$ otherwise.

Years_{it} = Number of years the present chief executive of firm i, in year t, has been the chief executive.

Because of the high multicollinearity that would result if profits and selling and administrative expense are used along with sales, a rate of return measure is substituted for level of profits, and selling and administrative expense as a fraction of sales is substituted for the level of selling and administrative expense. Both profits normalized by assets and profits normalized by common equity are used. The former measure provided stronger results. Selling and administrative expense as a fraction of size provides a measure of expenditure preference independent of firm size. If executives have a positive expense preference for staff and the firm has formulated an optimal compensation package, the sign of the elasticity of compensation with respect to staff should be negative.[19] All three independent variables are lagged one year to allow the compensation package to "react" to performance.

By using firm slope dummies, the analysis essentially becomes one of time series. Direct time series could not be used because some firms did not change their organization form over the sample period, and would therefore have caused the matrix of independent variables to be singular. It is worth noting that both U_{it} and M_{it} are able to be included because of the existence of some organizations other than the two "pure" forms. These other organizational forms are assigned a value of zero for both U_{it} and M_{it}.

Most previous studies of executive compensation have used cross-section data. These studies have generally observed that the level of executive compensation is related to some size variable. This result is hardly surprising. What these studies have concluded is a consequence of large firms having greater managerial needs than smaller firms. The large firm, in order to attract the talent it needs, must pay a greater price for its executives.[20]

The more interesting question, in a world similar to that described by Berle and Means, concerns the effects of compensation on managerial behavior. Once an executive is hired, is the executive's self interest (in this case increased compensation) increased by increases in firm sales or by increases in firm profitability? In order to answer a motivational question of this nature, time series data must be examined.

The log form of the estimating equations is chosen because each estimated coefficient measures the elasticity of compensation with respect to the independent variable in question. The statistical tests employed are similar to those used by Robert Masson.[21] After the regression coefficients are estimated using the pooled sample, the resulting estimates are compared for the nineteen firms in the sample. By using firm slope dummies, nineteen elasticities of executive compensation with respect to sales, rate of return, and selling and administrative expense as a percentage of sales are generated; one for each firm. These elasticities can be compared cross section by using the zero test.[2] The zero test gives the degree of confidence with which one can state that a sample of random numbers (in this case the elasticities) are not drawn from a population with a distribution with equal chance of drawing positive and negative numbers. As an example, look at the hypothesis that executive compensation increases with increases in the level of firm sales. If there is no relationship between compensation and sales, b_{1i} will be zero. Looking at equation 2-1 and the definition of compensation that includes only salary plus bonus, it is seen that nineteen of the coefficients are positive. Since there is no sample bias that would lead one to expect any elasticity to be either positive or negative and such a strong positive result is forthcoming, the hypothesis that compensation (at least with this definition) and sales are unrelated must be rejected. The chance of obtaining nineteen of nineteen positive coefficients from a neutral population is more than one in a thousand. The null hypothesis can be rejected at the .999 confidence level.

The results obtained from the zero test of the estimated coefficients of equation 2-1 are displayed in tables 2-1a and 2-1b. Equation 2-1 was estimated for all four definitions of compensation. Zero tests were performed for each equation for both the set of all coefficients and for the set of significant coefficients. The results with all coefficients and those with only significant coefficients are substantially the same in all cases. Only the results for TREM (salary + bonus + deferred income + retirement benefits) are discussed in the text. This definition includes every element of the compensation package which has a value unrelated to *ex post* firm performance. The COMPN and CMPN definitions include the value of stock options. These values were calculated by comparing the value of the stock at the time an option was exercised with the option price. The value of a firm's stock in the short run depends on many variables, some of which are not closely tied to firm

Table 2-1a. Comparison of Signs of Estimated Coefficients
from Equation 2-1 with Rate of Return on
Assets as the Profitability Measure

I	II		III	IV	V		VI
	+	-			+	-	
REMUN	19	0	.999	19	19	0	.999
TREM	19	0	.999	19	19	0	.999
COMPN	19	0	.999	19	19	0	.999
CMPN	19	0	.999	19	19	0	.999

Column I   Compensation Definition
Column II   Signs of b_{1i}
Column III   Zero Test Confidence Level
Column IV   Number of b_{1i} at 10% Significance
Column V   Signs of Significant b_{1i}
Column VI   Zero Test Confidence Level

I	II		III	IV	V		VI
	+	-			+	-	
REMUN	14	5	.990	11	8	3	.967
TREM	13	6	.968	12	9	3	.981
COMPN	16	3	.999	9	9	0	.998
CMPN	14	5	.990	8	7	1	.996

Column I   Compensation Definition
Column II   Signs of b_{2i}
Column III   Zero Test Confidence Level
Column IV   Number of b_{2i} at 10% Significance
Column V   Signs of Significant b_{2i}
Column VI   Zero Test Confidence Level

performance. Changes in these variables can cause short-run fluctuations in stock price which also can have a strong effect on the valuation of stock options. In terms of this study, it is important to differentiate between a change in compensation due to a change in firm policy and a change in compensation due to a change in firm performance. It is the former with which this study is concerned.

The relationship between executive compensation and firm sales is shown to be positive and extremely significant. Nineteen of the nineteen firms have estimates of the coefficient significant at the .10 level. All nineteen estimates are positive. If the nineteen estimates are considered to form a sample population, confidence intervals around the sample mean can be

Table 2-1b. Comparison of Signs of Estimated Coefficients
from Equation 2-1 with Rate of Return on
Equity as the Profitability Measure

I	II		III	IV	V		VI
	+	-			+	-	
REMUN	19	0	.999	19	19	0	.999
TREM	19	0	.999	19	19	0	.999
COMPN	19	0	.999	19	19	0	.999
CMPN	19	0	.999	19	19	0	.999

Column I   Compensation Definition
Column II   Signs of b_{1i}
Column III   Zero Test Confidence Level
Column IV   Number of b_{1i} at 10% Significance
Column V   Signs of Significant b_{1i}
Column VI   Zero Test Confidence Level

I	II		III	IV	V		VI
	+	-			+	-	
REMUN	12	7	.916	10	6	4	.828
TREM	11	8	.820	11	6	5	.725
COMPN	7	12	.180	8	2	6	.145
CMPN	7	12	.180	7	2	5	.226

Column I   Compensation Definition
Column II   Signs of b_{2i}
Column III   Zero Test Confidence Level
Column IV   Number of b_{2i} at 10% Significance
Column V   Signs of Significant b_{2i}
Column VI   Zero Test Confidence Level

formulated. Table 2-3a shows that the estimate of the elasticity of executive compensation with respect to sales is 0.45. The .95 confidence interval for this estimate ranges from 0.38 to 0.52. These results point strongly to a positive, but inelastic relationship between executive compensation and firm sales.

The same exercise is repeated for the estimate of the coefficient of the profitability term. Again TREM is the compensation definition which is discussed. These results are from the regression which uses return on assets as the profitability measure. Thirteen of the nineteen firms have positive coefficients. The zero test shows that a positive relationship between compensation and profitability can be asserted with a confidence level of .968. Of the nineteen estimates, twelve are significant at the .10 level, with nine of the twelve significant estimates being positive. The estimate of this elasticity is

0.23, with a .95 confidence interval from 0.01 to 0.45. Again, a strong, positive, inelastic relationship exists, this time between executive compensation and profitability.

In terms of the goals of this study, it is important to look at the changes attributed to organization form. For all four definitions of compensation, the coefficient of the dummy variable M_{it} is positive, however, only in the TREM equation is it significant even at the .10 level. The coefficient of U_{it} is negative and significant at the .01 level for the REMUN and TREM definitions and insignificant for the COMPN and CMPN definitions. Also note that for the REMUN and TREM definitions the coefficient of the YEARS variable is positive and significant at the .01 level. It is positive for both the COMPN definition and the CMPN definition, however neither estimate is significant. These results suggest that after sales, profitability and length of service are accounted for, the effect of the multidivisional form of organization is to increase the level of compensation of the chief executive officer.

Tables 2-2a and 2-2b display the same information for Equation 2 that tables 2-1a and 2-1b display for Equation 2-1. Equation 2-2 includes all the variables in Equation 2-1 with $\log(\text{Sell X}/\text{Sales})_{t-1}$ added. The results are similar. Using the zero test, the coefficient of $\log(\text{Sales})_{t-1}$ is seen to be positive and highly significant. Again, the results are essentially the same when the zero test is performed on only those estimates that are significant at the .10 level. The estimated mean of the elasticity with respect to sales in this equation is 0.43. The .95 confidence level is from 0.37 to 0.49.

The elasticity estimate for $\log(\text{Sell X}/\text{Sales})_{t-1}$ lends some support for the hierarchy model proposed by Simon. The zero test results show the elasticity estimates to be positive and significant. The estimated mean of the elasticities, however, is only 0.03 with a .95 confidence interval from 0.01 to 0.05.

The statistical tests which use equations 2-1 and 2-2 make the assumption that the elasticities of executive compensation with respect to sales, profitability, and selling expense do not differ between U-form firms and M-form firms. The dummy variables which account for differences in organization form measure the effect of the difference after the effects of sales, profitability, and selling expense are accounted for. That is, dummy variables show only a difference in the vertical intercepts of the regression lines for the organizational forms but not a difference in slopes. Equations 2-3 and 2-4 test for a difference in the elasticities. The previous method of looking at each firm in time series is not possible since many firms had only one organization form over the sample period. Therefore a pooled cross-section, time-series sample is used in making these tests. The equations used in making the tests are:

2-3: $\text{EC} = d_0 + d_1\text{SALESU} + d_2\text{SALESM}$

$$+ d_3\text{RRU} + d_4\text{RRM} + d_5\text{YEARS}$$

2-4: $EC = e_0 + e_1 SALESU + e_2 SALESM + e_3 RRU$
$+ e_4 RRM + e_5 PSELLU + e_6 PSELLM$
$+ e_7 YEARS$

where:

EC	$=$	executive compensation. The REMUN, TREM, COMPN, and CMPN definitions were used;
SALESU and SALESM	$=$	the sales of U-form and M-form firms respectively;
RRU and RRM	$=$	the profitability of U-form and M-form firms respectively. Profitability is measured both as the rate of return on assets and the rate of return on equity;
PSELLU and PSELLM	$=$	the selling and administrative expense as a percentage of sales for U-form and M-form firms respectively;
YEARS	$=$	the number of years the incumbent has served as the chief executive in the firm;

d_i $(i = 0, 5)$ and e_i $(i = 0, 7)$ are coefficients to be estimated.

The results of these tests are reported in appendix B. The results over the various definitions of executive compensation and profitability are similar. Looking at the equations using rate of return on assets as the profitability measure, there is little difference between the elasticity of executive compensation with respect to profitability in the U-form firms and that in the M-form firms. M-form firms, however, exhibit higher elasticities with respect to sales than do U-form firms. For firms of both organizational forms, the elasticity with respect to profitability is substantially higher than the elasticity with respect to sales. These results suggest that M-form management is given an incentive system which, while being as sensitive to current profitability as the management of U-form firms, also provides incentives which reward growth. This is consistent with the results reported by Weston and Mansinghka.[23] They found that conglomerate firms improved the performance (including profitability) of poorly performing firms. Since M-form firms acquired many new divisions during the sample period, the desire

Table 2-2a. Comparison of Signs of Estimated Coefficients from Equation 2-2 with Rate of Return on Assets as the Profitability Measure

I	II +	II -	III	IV	V +	V -	VI
REMUN	19	0	.999	19	19	0	.999
TREM	19	0	.999	19	19	0	.999
COMPN	19	0	.999	19	19	0	.999
CMPN	19	0	.999	19	19	0	.999

Column I Compensation Definition
Column II Signs of c_{1i}
Column III Zero Test Confidence Level
Column IV Number of c_{1i} at 10% Significance
Column V Signs of Significant c_{1i}
Column VI Zero Test Confidence Level

I	II +	II -	III	IV	V +	V -	VI
REMUN	13	6	.967	10	7	3	.944
TREM	13	6	.967	11	7	4	.887
COMPN	16	3	.998	9	9	0	.998
CMPN	14	5	.990	7	7	0	.992

Column I Compensation Definition
Column II Signs of c_{2i}
Column III Zero Test Confidence Level
Column IV Number of c_{2i} at 10% Significance
Column V Signs of Significant c_{2i}
Column VI Zero Test Confidence Level

I	II +	II -	III	IV	V +	V -	VI
REMUN	13	6	.967	3	3	0	.875
TREM	13	6	.967	4	4	0	.937
COMPN	15	4	.998	6	5	1	.948
CMPN	15	4	.998	4	2	2	.500

Column I Compensation Definition
Column II Signs of c_{3i}
Column III Zero Test Confidence Level
Column IV Number of c_{3i} at 10% Significance
Column V Signs of Significant c_{3i}
Column VI Zero Test Confidence Level

Table 2-2b. Comparison of Signs of Estimated Coefficients from Equation 2-2 with Rate of Return on Equity as the Profitability Measure

I	II +	II -	III	IV	V +	V -	VI
REMUN	19	0	.999	19	19	0	.999
TREM	19	0	.999	19	19	0	.999
COMPN	19	0	.999	19	19	0	.999
CMPN	19	0	.999	19	19	0	.999

Column I   Compensation Definition
Column II   Signs of c_{1i}
Column III   Zero Test Confidence Level
Column IV   Number of c_{1i} at 10% Significance
Column V   Signs of Significant c_{1i}
Column VI   Zero Test Confidence Level

I	II +	II -	III	IV	V +	V -	VI
REMUN	9	10	.500	11	7	3	.944
TREM	12	7	.917	11	6	5	.725
COMPN	7	12	.180	7	3	4	.500
CMPN	7	12	.180	8	3	5	.363

Column I   Compensation Definition
Column II   Signs of c_{2i}
Column III   Zero Test Confidence Level
Column IV   Number of c_{2i} at 10% Significance
Column V   Signs of Significant c_{2i}
Column VI   Zero Test Confidence Level

I	II +	II -	III	IV	V +	V -	VI
REMUN	14	5	.990	5	5	0	.969
TREM	14	5	.990	6	6	0	.984
COMPN	13	6	.967	4	4	0	.937
CMPN	13	0	.967	3	3	0	.875

Column I   Compensation Definition
Column II   Signs of c_{3i}
Column III   Zero Test Confidence Level
Column IV   Number of c_{3i} at 10% Significance
Column V   Signs of Significant c_{3i}
Column VI   Zero Test Confidence Level

Table 2-3a. Means and Standard Deviations of Elasticity Estimates from Equation 2-1 with Various Definitions of Compensation with Rate of Return on Assets as the Measure of Profitability

Elasticity Measure	Compensation Measure	Mean	Standard Deviation
b_1	REMUN	.43	.17
b_1	TREM	.45	.16
b_1	COMPN	.51	.17
b_1	CMPN	.57	.23
b_2	REMUN	.17	.46
b_2	TREM	.23	.50
b_2	COMPN	.33	.47
b_2	CMPN	.36	.61

where: b_1 — percent change in compensation for a percent change in sales

b_2 = percent change in compensation for a percent change in profitability

Table 2-3b. Means and Standard Deviations of Elasticity Estimates from Equation 2-1 with Various Definitions of Compensation with Rate of Return on Equity as the Measure of Profitability

Elasticity Measure	Compensation Measure	Mean	Standard Deviation
b_1	REMUN	.52	.15
b_1	TREM	.52	.16
b_1	COMPN	.66	.17
b_1	CMPN	.77	.30
b_2	REMUN	.10	.53
b_2	TREM	.10	.56
b_2	COMPN	-.08	.61
b_2	CMPN	-.03	.92

where: b_1 = percent change in compensation for a percent change in sales

b_2 = percent change in compensation for a percent change in profitability

Table 2-4a.   Means and Standard Deviations of Elasticity
Estimates from Equation 2-2 with Various Definitions of
Compensation with Rate of Return on Assets
as the Measure of Profitability

Elasticity Measure	Compensation Measure	Mean	Standard Deviation
b_1	REMUN	.43	.17
b_1	TREM	.43	.15
b_1	COMPN	.44	.19
b_1	CMPN	.51	.30
b_2	REMUN	.17	.46
b_2	TREM	.21	.49
b_2	COMPN	.37	.48
b_2	CMPN	.44	.68
b_3	REMUN	.03	.04
b_3	TREM	.03	.05
b_3	COMPN	.04	.08
b_3	CMPN	.03	.10

where: b_1 =   percent change in compensation for a percent change in sales

b_2 =   percent change in compensation for a percent change in profitability

b_3 =   percent change in compensation for a percent change in selling and administrative expense normalized by sales

of M-form firms to acquire firms with the capacity for improvement would explain this result.

The results from equation 2-4 show that M-form firms have incentive systems which better attenuate staff expansion biases. The results for the elasticities with respect to sales and profitability are similar to those from equation 2-3. However, the M-form firms are much more successful in penalizing excessive spending for staff. For every definition of executive compensation, the elasticity with respect to selling and administrative expense is lower for M-form firms than for U-form firms. The REMUN and TREM definitions of executive compensation have negative and significant elasticity estimates for M-form firms. The COMPN and CMPN definitions have low positive and insignificant estimates. For M-form firms the executive compensation definitions which are more short term in nature (REMUN and

Table 2-4b.   Means and Standard Deviations of Elasticity
Estimates from Equation 2-2 with Various Definitions
of Compensation with Rate of Return on Equity
as the Measure of Profitability

Elasticity Measure	Compensation Measure	Mean	Standard Deviation
b_1	REMUN	.51	.16
b_1	TREM	.50	.16
b_1	COMPN	.59	.20
b_1	CMPN	.72	.34
b_2	REMUN	.10	.55
b_2	TREM	.07	.58
b_2	COMPN	-.001	.64
b_2	CMPN	.04	.97
b_3	REMUN	.03	.05
b_3	TREM	.04	.05
b_3	COMPN	.04	.07
b_3	CMPN	.03	.08

where: b_1 = percent change in compensation for a percent change in sales

b_2 = percent change in compensation for a percent change in profitability

b_3 = percent change in compensation for a percent change in selling and administrative expense normalized by sales

TREM) penalize excessive spending on staff, while those more long term in nature (COMPN and CMPN) are neutral. Since most stock options are exercised after the executive has left office and the executive should not show a long-term staff expense bias, this is a compensation package which is of the form one would expect from a firm trying to attenuate non-profit-maximizing behavior. In this regard, note the higher elasticities with respect to profitability for M-form firms among the longer-term definitions. This further demonstrates a compensation package directed towards increasing long-run profitability.[24]

Conclusions

The results of the zero test indicate that the compensation package of the top executive is determined in a complex fashion. Size of the firm, return on capital, and size of staff all show significant positive relationships to compensation. As was discussed, a compensation package that is designed to maximize profit should have a positive relationship between profit and compensation. Other variables, such as level of sales and size of staff, which the executive might pursue for his own personal or professional benefit and which do not contribute to higher profitability, should have a negative relation to compensation. The cost to the executive of increasing staff, as an example, should be just enough compared to the benefit to the executive of increasing profits that staff is expanded to its profit-maximizing level. A profit-maximizing compensation package of this nature was not discovered in the tests utilizing equations 2-1 and 2-2. These results do not demonstrate that there is no firm which maintains such a package. Recall that the statistical technique used a pooling of time series results over nineteen firms.

A second series of statistical tests dropped the assumption of equal elasticities for U-form and M-form firms. These tests show similar elasticities of compensation with respect to profitability in U-form and M-form firms. However, elasticities are higher in M-form firms with respect to sales than in U-form firms. M-form firms provide a compensation package which penalize staff expansion bias more than do those of U-form firms. It is concluded that the compensation package in the M-form firm is similar to that which would be expected in a firm highly concerned with long-run profitability.

Like those of Lewellen and Huntsman,[25] the results of this study are stronger statistically when stock options are excluded from the definition of compensation. The reason that the more inclusive definition gives poorer results can be attributed to the method by which stock options are valued. Other elements in the compensation package have a set value at the time they are issued. That is, these other elements do not depend on *ex post* behavior (by either the executive or the firm). The value of a stock option depends on both the length of the period between the date on which it is granted and the date on which it is exercised and the performance of the stock during this period. The date on which an option is exercised is often influenced by factors which are exogenous to the model discussed. The ability of the executive to raise the capital needed to exercise the option is included among these factors. The performance of a firm's stock, while strongly influenced by management, is also subject to influence by factors independent of any management control. The most obvious of these factors is the general state of the economy.

Stock options are issued sporadically. An attempt was made to identify the factors that determine the timing and amount of issuance. The only relationship that is possible to identify is the tendency of firms to grant options to a new president. No measure of firm performance showed itself to have a significant relationship with the timing of the granting of stock options.

The results give support to several of the theoretical models discussed in an earlier section of this paper. The strong positive relationships between both sales and rate of return to compensation is consistent with the neoclassical model. As inputs other than executive management are increased, the marginal product of the executive reflects the increase in marginal product. The level of sales is a good proxy for the size of the firm and therefore is a good proxy for the level of inputs. Similarly an increase in the firm's rate of return reflects an increase in the executive's marginal product. Without perfect mobility, the executive is unable to capture all of his marginal product. Part of the marginal product goes towards increased compensation, and part goes to increased firm profit.

The positive relationships between sales and compensation, staff and compensation, and the M-form organization and compensation are all consistent with the previously discussed organizational theory advocated by Herbert Simon. Simon posits that compensation is determined by the number of levels of bureaucracy in the firm. If sales and staff are viewed as having positive relationships with the number of levels of bureaucracy, then Simon's theory predicts the positive relationships that are observed. The M-form organization, in its simplest form, is made up of profit centers, which are organized along functional lines. The activities of the profit centers are coordinated and monitored by a superstructure of corporate staff members and top corporate executives. Remembering that Simon does not discuss the size of each bureaucratic level, it is reasonable to assume that the functional profit centers have approximately the same number of levels as the U-form firm. If this assumption holds, the divisional head will have a salary similar to that of the chief executive of the U-form firm. Using Simon's notation, the chief executive of the M-form firm will have a salary b times that of his U-form equivalent.

In terms of the overall goals of this study, the most important results are those using equation 2-4. These are the results which show that M-form firms offer a compensation package more nearly like that of a profit maximizer than do U-form firms. Statistically, the results are very strong. All elasticity estimates are highly significant. The results are of the form predicted by the multidivisional form hypothesis.

3

The Effect of Organization Form on Profitability

The Multidivision Hypothesis does not explicitly address issues such as the determination of dividend levels or the amount of compensation that executives receive. While these issues play important roles in the construction of the multidivision hypothesis, its conclusion is stated in terms of the firm's profitability. This chapter studies the effect the adoption of a multidivisional (M-form) organization has on a firm's profitability.

As a firm expands and diversifies it becomes more vulnerable to the problems of subgoal pursuit by its employees. These goals often are not consistent with the overall goals of the firm. In addition, the firm experiences a decreased ability to monitor and control the behavior of its units. Williamson[1] summarizes the argument as: "The transformation of a large business firm for which divisionalization is feasible from a unitary to a multidivisional form organization contributes to (but does not assure) an attenuation of both the control-loss experience and subgoal pursuit (mainly staff-biased expansion) that are characteristic of the unitary form." Stated more formally: "The organization and operation of the large enterprise along the lines of the M-form favors goal-pursuit and least-cost behavior more nearly associated with the neoclassical profits-maximization hypothesis than does the U-form organizational alternative."[2]

Statistical Models

In this section, several statistical tests of the M-form hypothesis are discussed. For each firm in the test sample, time series analyses of its profitability are conducted. After standard explanatory variables are used to account for the level of a firm's profitability, tests are conducted to see how the change to an M-form organization affected that firm's profitability. While each of the different statistical tests examines the multidivisional hypothesis in a slightly different way, the question that dominates the analysis is: How much has the firm's rate of return improved, compared to the rate of return of a previously selected standard, after the adoption of the M-form organization? The standard to which the firm's profitability is compared is designed to measure how well similar firms have done during the period. If the multidivision hypothesis is correct, then it is expected that the profitability of the firm will increase, *ceteris paribus,* after the M-form organization is in place.

These statistical tests are similar to those used by Weston and Mansinghka in their study of conglomerate performance.[3] They compared the performance of conglomerate firms with that of a random sample for both 1958 and 1968. They found that in 1958 the rates of return for conglomerate firms were lower than the rate of return for the random sample and that the difference between these rates of return was statistically significant. By 1968 this difference and its significance had disappeared. They concluded that, "It appears, therefore, that an important economic function of conglomerate firms has been raising the profitability of firms with depressed earnings to the average for industry generally."[4]

In many ways the multidivisional hypothesis can be restated in a fashion similar to the Weston-Mansinghka conclusion. No claim is made that the M-form organization is superior to the U-form organization for all firms. Simple, non-diversified tasks are seen as being performed efficiently by a functional form of organization. It is suggested, however, that as a firm grows and diversifies, its old functional organization becomes inadequate for the complex tasks inherent in a large diversified firm.[5] Unless a firm is able to perceive instantaneously the need for a new form of organization, it is expected to perform, for a time, at a level that is less than optimal. As the problems caused by the functional organization grow, so do the pressures to adopt an organization of the M-form type.[6] If this scenario is correct, it is expected that the profitability of firms adopting M-form organizations should improve in the years following its adoption compared to the profitability of a more general standard.

Several statistical tests are conducted in testing the M-form hypothesis. Each of these tests is generated from the basic model discussed above. The difference between the firm's profitability and the profitability of a general sample is compared at the time the firm changed to the M-form organization and again in later years. If the M-form hypothesis is correct, then it is expected that this difference will have increased. The firm's rate of return on equity is the measure of profitability which is used. Return on equity is chosen because it is what would be maximized by managers if they were attempting to maximize stockholder welfare. Regressions are run for each firm using a sample of the years 1954-72. The independent variables include variables of the type normally used to explain firm profitability. These include size, financing, and diversification measures. Because "market structure" variables are incorporated into the standard used for comparison, they are not introduced again into the analysis. Any change in market structure affects the performance of the standard as well as that of the firm.

A sample of twenty-seven firms is used.[7] These twenty-seven firms all come from the original group of the 250 largest industrial firms (1972 *Fortune 500*). They are the firms for which complete data are available for the 1954-72 period, and for which it is possible to state with confidence that the firm adopted the M-form organization between 1954 and 1967.

Two different methods are used to measure the firm's profitability under the M-form organization. One is to introduce dummy variables with a value of one into the regression for those years when the firm used an M-form organization. The other is to compare regression residuals five years after the M-form organization is in place with those from the year in which it was adopted. The first method compares the firm's profitability for the complete M-form period with its profitability for the complete U-form period. This method does not distinguish between optimal and non-optimal choices of organization form. The second method compares the firm's experience with the M-form organization with its latest experience with the U-form organization. Both methods only examine firms with at least five years of experience with an M-form organization.

It is felt that five years under the new organization provides a good test period. Several factors contribute to this decision. The first is simply that a longer lag eliminates too many firms from the sample. Even when five years is used as the test period, only twenty-seven firms remain to be tested. Second, five years seems to be a long enough period for the firm to work out most of the problems associated with the new organization form. Last, if top management used the extra profits generated by the organization change for personal discretionary spending,[8] it is unlikely to have occurred immediately since the increased profits may turn out to be temporary. If the profits generated by the change to the M-form organization are used to increase top-level executive compensation, reported profit levels will not reflect the increased efficiencies of the type hypothesized by the M-form hypothesis. If the increased profitability does take the form of increased compensation for top executives, the dummy variable method will not show the increased profitability. However, the increased profitability will be identified by the residual test. Five years seems long enough for the increased profitability which would be associated with the M-form organization to appear, yet short enough that top management may still not regard the profits as permanent, and thus, not allocate the profits to themselves.[9]

Because it is not commonly used, a further explanation of the residual method should be helpful. Under the usual assumptions of the regression model, the expected value of the residual in each year is zero. If the M-form hypothesis is correct, after accounting for variations in firm profitability due to the usual explanations, the expected value of the residual in each year is not zero. Rather, the value of the residual should be higher in the years after the implementation of the M-form organization. For each firm the residual in the first year the M-form organization is used ($t = T$) is compared with the residual five years later ($t = T + 5$). Since the sum of expected values equals the expected value of the sum, the expected value of the difference between the residuals in time $t = T$ and $t = T + 5$ is zero if the regression is properly specified and the M-form hypothesis should be rejected. Zero tests are used to test whether the expected value of this difference equals zero. The difference between the residual in the fifth year after the adoption of the M-form and the residual in the year of the adoption are computed for each of the twenty-seven firms in the sample. If the M-form hypothesis should be rejected, then the number of firms having a positive difference between these residuals should be approximately equal to the number of firms having a negative difference between the residuals. If the M-form hypothesis is correct, the great majority of firms should have a positive difference between these two residuals.

Before examining the actual specifications which are used in the regression models, it should be helpful to discuss reasons why these methods of testing may fail to identify increased profitability of the type suggested by the M-form hypothesis, even when this increased profitability occurred. These statistical tests assume that the firm does not adopt the M-form organization until some time after growth and diversification have made the M-form the superior form of organization. The tests assume that an adaptive response occurs after the firm views its profitability falling to unacceptable levels. The year the M-form organization is adopted is used as the base year to see if the firms profitability improves. If a U-form organization is replaced by a M-form organization at the optimal time (and not several years later), the base year will not have unacceptable levels of profitability, and hence, the statistical tests will not show increased profitability resulting when the M-form is adopted, even if the M-form hypothesis is correct.

A second possible problem is that firms may have prematurely adopted the M-form organization. If a firm with a narrow set of products splits up these products into individual profit centers, there is a chance that this change will cause its profitability to fall. The individual profit centers will cause unnecessary duplication of effort in cases where the closeness of the products allows functions to be combined (e.g., sales forces). The divisions may be too small to be efficient profit centers. It is possible that some firms which contributed results with negative signs adopted the M-form organization prematurely. The statistical tests do not distinguish between firms which adopted the M-form organization prematurely and those which did not.

A third reason why these tests may not pick up increased profitability involves the use of return on equity. If stock prices immediately reflect any effects of an M-form organization the value of equity will rise. As a result, the profitability measure will not indicate the increased profits. While this effect may cause problems in testing very long-term relationships, it should not have a profound effect on this study. Stock prices do not fully discount events which are perceived to be transitory. Since all firms in each industry did not adopt the M-form organization at the same time, there is apparently a learning period of some length. If people in the industry require a long learning period, it is unlikely that most people outside the industry will learn quicker. Thus, it is unlikely that stock prices will fully reflect increased profitability due to the M-form organization, and, as a result, return on equity should show the increased profitability.

Model 1 (IRR): Comparison to Industry Rate of Return

Two forms of the regression model are used to test the hypothesis. Both forms compare the firm's rate of return over time with the rate of return of a standard. The first form (IRR) uses as its dependent variable the difference between the firm's rate of return and the rate of return of those industries in which the firm is a member. The industry rates of return are weighted for each firm by the percentage of the firm's sales derived from each industry.

Some problems are inherent in this model. Industry rate of return data were obtained from *Standard & Poor's Industry Studies*. The statistic which is reported is return on book value. Each industry's return is a weighted average of the returns of its largest members. Since the firms being tested are inevitably among the largest, the two values which are constructed to form the dependent variable are not structurally independent of each other. When the rate of return of the firm being tested increases, the rate of return of its industries necessarily increases, although by a fraction of the increase for the firm. Accuracy of the data is a second problem. For many of the firms, accurate data which break sales down by major industry do not exist. This problem is particularly acute for the years before 1966, since post-1966 data are available from the firms' 10-K reports.[10] Estimates for the earlier years are made by extrapolating backward with the help of annual reports, business magazines, data obtained from the firms, and interviews with executives of the firm. However, since most of the firms did not engaged in major diversification until the mid-1960s, this problem is not as severe as it might seem. This problem, moreover, does not bias the results. The statistical significance of the results, however, will be understated. That is, the tendency is to accept the hypothesis of equal rates of return between the firm and its industries even when the hypothesis is false.

Model 2 (CAPM): Capital Asset Pricing Model

The second form of the regression model closely resembles the Capital Asset Pricing Model (CAPM).[11] CAPM examines the equilibrium relationship between a security's (or firm's) expected return and the expected return of the market portfolio. This relationship is defined as:

$$(3\text{-}1) \qquad E(R_i) = R_f + \beta_i \, [E(R_m) - R_f]$$

where:

$$E(R_i) \quad = \quad \text{expected return for the } ith \text{ firm}$$

$$E(R_m) \quad = \quad \text{expected return for the market portfolio}$$

$$R_f \quad = \quad \text{risk free interest rate}$$

$$\beta_i \quad = \quad \text{coefficient to be estimated. } \beta_i \text{ is a}$$
measure of the correlation between the firm's return and the market's return

If this equation is changed slightly, then it becomes possible to use the model to test the M-form hypothesis.

$$(3\text{-}2) \qquad E(R_i) - R_f = a_i + \beta \, [E(R_m) - R_f]$$

is equation (3-1) with an intercept term added. The intercept term, a_i, is the difference in the ith firm's rate of return compared to a portfolio based on the total market with equal systematic risk. Systematic risk is that part of the firm's risk which is due to changes in the performance of the total market. Unsystematic risk is that part of the firm's risk which is due to random shocks peculiar to the specific firm.

Like the previous model, CAPM is estimated by ordinary least squares, so that the expected value of the residuals from the regression is equal to zero when the equation is specified properly. Using the same procedure which was employed with the previous model, the residual from the regression in the year the M-form organization was adopted ($t = T$) is compared with the residual five years later ($t = T + 5$). If the M-form hypothesis is correct, this difference should be positive for most firms.

Expansions of the Models

Besides the two basic forms of the regression model, additional explanatory variables are added in an attempt to account for the variance in the firm's profitability which is explained by neither cyclical movements of its industries nor a change in organization form. Each of these additional explanatory variables can be categorized as being "firm" variables. That is, they measure differences in the conduct of the firm and do not measure changes in market structure. Presumably changes in market structure will affect all firms in an industry and thus will be picked up by both the firm's and the industry's rate of return.

The first of the additional explanatory variables to be introduced is sales. As firms grow larger and more complex the difficulties of the U-form organization become more pronounced. As Chandler points out:

> The inherent weakness in the centralized, functionally departmentalized operating company ... became critical only when the administrative load on the senior executives increased to such an extent that they were unable to handle their entrepreneurial responsibilities efficiently. This situation arose when the operations of the enterprise became too complex and the problems of coordination, appraisal, and policy formulation too intricate for a small number of top officers to handle both long-run entrepreneurial, and short-run operational administrative activities. [12]

As the firm became larger and more complex, top management became unable to effectively coordinate and monitor the operating segments of the firm. In addition, people working in the operating segments of the firm became either unwilling or unable to recognize and work towards the goals of the firm. Long-run goals of the firm were replaced with shorter-run local goals of the particular operating unit.

Problems of the type associated with size are compounded when that size is reached quickly. Whatever ability the firm's organization has in solving such problems is weakened when that change happens suddenly. For this reason a growth variable is introduced. The absolute change in sales and the percentage change in sales are the growth measures used.

Problems of specification of goals, coordination of operating and strategic planning, and monitoring of operating units are also compounded by increasing diversification. Chandler categorized the problems which DuPont experienced after its diversification:

> Broad goals and policies had to be determined for and resources allocated to functional activities, not in one industry but in several. Appraisal of departments performing in diverse fields became exceedingly complex. Interdepartmental coordination grew comparably more complex. [13]

Measurement of diversification is rather difficult. Several measures have been proposed as ways to measure a firm's diversification. The most straightforward is a simple count of industries in which the firm participates. This measure is deficient in that it does not consider the share of the firm's total activities accounted for by each industry. A second measure is the reciprocal of the firm's product specialization. The reciprocal of product specialization measures the portion of a firm's sales accounted for by its major industry. This measure fails to consider how the firm's sales are distributed among its non-leading industries. A third measure of diversification, the Herfindahl index, does account for the distribution of sales throughout the firm. The major conceptual problem with the Herfindahl index is that it is sensitive to the price of the firm's goods. For the purposes of this study changes in price should not affect the extent of the firm's diversification. A second problem with the Herfindahl Index is that sales data at a properly disaggregated level within the firm are usually not available. All these measures suffer from their inability to define the proper level of disaggregation at which to define an industry.

A recent study[14] took these diversification measures, plus two others, and compared them using Spearman rank correlation. The authors concluded that all of the indexes are closely related. Because of the strength of this result and because other data are very difficult to obtain, the number of four-digit SIC industries in which the firm performed is the measure of diversification which is used.

Because the firm's performance is being measured by its rate of return on equity, its debt-equity ratio is included as an independent variable.[15] As Hall and Weiss point out, the firm's capital structure can be considered to be an element of its input mix.[16] This is consistent with the theorem derived by Modigliani and Miller dealing with financial risk.[17] They show that, "The expected yield of a share of stock is equal to the appropriate capitalization rate for the stock were the company financed entirely with equity (i.e., K_e (for unleveraged stock) $\equiv k_o$) plus a premium related to financial risk equal to the debt-to-equity ratio times the spread between k_o and k_i (the interest rate)." This can be represented symbolically as:

$$k_e = k_o + (k_o - k_i)D/S$$

where:

k_e = rate of return on equity

k_o = rate of return on equity if the firm were financed entirely with equity

k_i = the interest rate the firm must pay for its debt

D = the value of the firm's long-term debt

S = the value of the firm's equity

Results

A review of the results from the models described above show similar trends. The cross-section comparisons of the twenty-seven firms which adopted an M-form organization are remarkably similar from model to model. Not one model, or modification, generated differences in the results, which are significantly different from the random result. Interestingly, when the results from the various models were correlated with each other, high levels of correlation were found. Since the results are derived from models which have different structural forms and test the hypothesis in different ways, high correlations are not expected unless the results are accurately reflecting the firms' behavior.

A further examination of the results shows the existence of two patterns which give some support for the M-form hypothesis. The first is that firms adopting the M-form organization in the later years of the sample are much more likely to have improved their performance five years later than are firms which adopted the M-form organization during the early years of the sample. This pattern is consistent with the notion that an organizational innovation, like more traditional forms of innovation, needs a period of learning before it is able to work to its potential.

A second pattern may be more important. Among those firms having negative residuals in the year the M-form organization was adopted, a large majority had improved their performance five years later. Since the expected value of the residual in any year (including $t = T + 5$) is equal to zero, this tendency is expected even if the M-form hypothesis should be rejected. The results, however, apparently are greater than would occur randomly. Since the M-form innovation is usually viewed as an adaptive response to a decline in corporate performance, it is firms with negative residuals which are expected to improve their performance with the adoption of the M-form organization.

Results: The Basic Models

To review, two basic models are used to test the effect an M-form organization has on a firm's profitability. The first model (IRR) uses the difference between the firm's rate of return and the rate of return of a weighted average of its industries as the dependent variable. The second model (CAPM) is a variation of the capital asset pricing model. The two models were expanded to account for variations in each firm's sales, changes in sales, financial structure, and diversification. Each model measures the effect of the M-form organization in two ways. One way compares, for each firm, the residual of the regression in the year the M-form organization was adopted with the residual five years later. The other way uses dummy variables to compare each firm's profitability with an M-form organization and with other types of organization. For both methods, the results are then compared across all firms in the sample. If the M-form hypothesis is to be accepted, the number of firms having a positive effect should be significantly greater than would occur randomly. The results are reported in tables 3-1a, 3-1b, 3-2a, and 3-2b.

Table 3-1a.   Signs of Residuals from IRR and its Variations

Model	Total Number of Firms	Number of Firms with Positive Residuals	Average of Residuals*
IRR	27	15	-58.4
IRRS	27	13	-13.2
IRRSDE	27	13	-13.0
IRRSDED	26	13	-63.6

where: IRR   =   Regression where dependent variable is the difference between the firm's rate of return and that of a weighted average of its industries

IRRS   =   IRR + sales

IRRSDE   =   IRRS + debt-equity ratio

IRRSDED   =   IRRSDE + diversification

*A value of 100 equals a rate of return of 1%

In all, eighteen different forms of the two models are examined. Besides the fourteen reported in tables 3-1a, 3-1b, 3-2a, and 3-2b, the basic models plus a growth variable were run. The results in these variations are almost the same as in the variation of the model where growth is replaced by the level of sales. In no case does a model produce results that are significantly different from the random result. The model which produces the greatest proportion of positive differences is the simple comparison between the firm's rate of return and a weighted average of rates of return of its industries. Fifteen of the twenty-seven firms have positive differences. This result would occur randomly one time in four. No other variation on the models produces a result in which there are a significantly greater number of positive residuals or coefficient estimates than negative residuals or coefficient estimates. The CAPM variation with the addition of a sales term produces twelve positive and fifteen negative residuals. The results are in the wrong direction and are not significantly different from the random result.

Table 3-1b. Signs of Dummy Variable Estimated Coefficients from IRR and Its Variations

Model	Total Number of Firms	Number of Firms with Positive Coefficient Estimates	Average of Coefficient Estimates*
IRR	27	10	- 56.8
IRRS	27	9	- 76.4
IRRSDE	27	8	-109.3
IRRSDED	26	11	- 94.6

where: IRR   =   Regression where dependent variable is the difference between the firm's rate of return and that of a weighted average of its industries

            IRRS   =   IRR + sales

          IRRSDE   =   IRRS + debt-equity ratio

        IRRSDED   =   IRRSDE + diversification

*A value of 100 equals a rate of return of 1%

Table 3-2a. Signs of Residuals from CAPM and Its Variations

Model	Total Number of Firms	Number of Firms with Positive Residuals	Average of Residuals*
CAPM	27	13	-32.2
CAPMS	27	12	-50.0
CAPMSD	26	14	-24.6

where: CAPM   =   Capital Asset Pricing Model

          CAPMS   =   CAPM + sales

       CAPMSD   =   CAPMS + diversification

*A value of 100 equals a rate of return of 1%

Table 3-2b.   Signs of Dummy Variable Estimated Coefficients
from CAPM and Its Variations

Model	Total Number of Firms	Number of Firms with Positive Coefficient Estimates	Average of Coefficient Estimates*
CAPM	27	8	-111.9
CAPMS	27	8	-102.9
CAPMSD	26	12	-146.7

where: CAPM   =   Capital Asset Pricing Model

CAPMS   =   CAPM + sales

CAPMSD   =   CAPMS + diversification

*A value of 100 equals a rate of return of 1%

Every other variation of the models using the residual method produces either thirteen or fourteen positive differences. Sales added to IRR produces thirteen positive differences, as does IRR plus sales plus the debt-equity plus diversification.[18] The simple CAPM form also produces thirteen positive differences. The addition of change in sales (either absolute change or percentage change) to CAPM produces fourteen positive differences, and when diversification is added to this model fourteen positive differences result.

The analyses which use dummy variables to indicate the presence of an M-form organization also failed to indicate a significant positive relationship between profitability and an M-form organization. Tables 3-1b and 3-2b show the results. They range from three model variations which show eight firms out of twenty-seven having positive estimates to one model variation showing twelve firms out of twenty-six having positive estimates. Also note that for every model variation the average of the coefficient estimates is negative.

One last series of tests are performed. For each of the models, the residual in the year the M-form organization was adopted is compared with the average of the firm's residuals for all years, starting five years after the organizational change. The results are substantially the same as the previous form of the test. Indeed, this test is similar to using a dummy variable with a five year lag to indicate the presence of an M-form organization. IRR produces ten positive differences (out of twenty-seven), IRR plus sales produces fourteen, CAPM produces thirteen, and CAPM plus sales produces fifteen.

Results: Correlations

While the IRR and CAPM models are designed to test the same hypothesis, they are different in form and use data which are quite different. This makes it unlikely that results generated from the two models would be highly correlated unless the correlation reflects an underlying relationship. Correlations are run over all the models to see if the results from the models are related. Tables 3-3a and 3-3b show the high degree of correlation between most results.

Table 3-3a.   Correlation Analysis of Differences Between Residuals
in Years T and T + 5 for Various Regression Models

	CAPM	CAPMS	CAPMDS	CAPMPS	IRR	IRRS	IRRSDE
CAPM	1.00	.87	.95	.94	.82	.82	.68
CAPMS	.87	1.00	.90	.88	.65	.68	.51
CAPMDS	.95	.90	1.00	.99	.70	.74	.56
CAPMPS	.94	.88	.99	1.00	.74	.79	.58
IRR	.82	.65	.70	.74	1.00	.95	.85
IRRS	.82	.68	.74	.79	.95	1.00	.87
IRRSDE	.68	.51	. 56	. 58	.85	.87	1.00

CAPM	=	Capital Asset Pricing Model
CAPMS	=	CAPM plus sales
CAPMDS	=	CAPM plus absolute change in sales
CAPMPS	=	CAPM plus percentage change in sales
IRR	=	Dependent variable is the difference between the firm's rate of return and that of its industries
IRSS	=	IRR plus sales
IRRSDE	=	IRR plus sales plus debt-equity ratio

Results: Observable Trends

There are two trends from the results of the models which may offer some insight into why some firms do better under the M-form organization than do other firms. Recall that the M-form hypothesis makes no claims for the superiority of the M-form organization under all conditions. Rather, the M-form hypothesis sees the new organization form as being an adaptive response to problems which result from the firm's growth and diversification. Chandler's

Table 3-3b.   Correlation Analysis of Estimated Coefficient of M-form
Dummy Variables for Various Regression Models

	CAPM	CAPMS	IRR	IRRS	IRRSDE
CAPM	1.00	.51	.80	.63	.50
CAPMS	.52	1.00	.57	.32	.20
IRR	.80	.57	1.00	.78	.70
IRRS	.63	.32	.78	1.00	.95
IRRSDE	.50	.20	.70	.95	1.00

CAPM	=	Capital Asset Pricing Model
CAPMS	=	CAPM plus sales
IRR	=	Dependent variable is the difference between the firm's rate of return and that of its industries
IRRS	=	IRR plus sales
IRRSDE	=	IRR plus sales plus debt-equity ratio

description of DuPont and General Motors shows that both firms adopted the M-form organization in response to problems associated with expansion.[19] The new form was adopted only after a period in which the firm performed at a subpar level. A proper test of the M-form hypothesis should include only those firms whose size and diversification make the M-form organization a superior form. If, as seems reasonable, it is assumed that the firm undergoes a period of subpar performance before it changes to the M-form organization, then those firms with negative residuals in the year the M-form organization was adopted seem to be good candidates for the test. The tests which were described previously are repeated for those firms with negative residuals in year T. With some small exceptions the residual form of the tests produced results consistent with the M-form hypothesis. The IRR form of the model produced ten firms (out of the twelve firms with negative residuals in year T) with positive differences between its residuals in years T and T + 5. IRR plus sales produced twelve (out of fifteen) positive differences, CAPM produced twelve (out of fourteen) positive differences, and CAPM plus sales produced twelve (out of eighteen) positive differences. Similar results are obtained when the test is changed to measure the difference between the residual in year T and the average of residuals for all years T + 5 and later. Using this average, IRR produced fourteen positive differences (out of fifteen negative residuals in year T), CAPM produced twelve (out of fourteen), and CAPM plus sales produced fourteen (out of eighteen).

The second observable trend involves the timing of the adoption of the M-form. Firms which adopted the M-form in the late 1960s did better in the test than firms adopting the form during the 1950s and early 1960s. It is possible that this reflects a better understanding of how best to employ the M-form among those firms which adopted the M-form later. Like most innovations, the M-form organization may require a period of learning, which can be shortened by observing the experiences of firms which adopted it previously.[20]

Summary and Conclusions

The purpose of this analysis is to test the multidivision hypothesis directly. This was done by looking at the results from two models and variations from these two models. Model 1 uses the difference between each firm's profitability and that of the industries in which it is engaged as the dependent variable. This difference in the year the M-form organization is adopted is compared with the same variable five years later. If the multidivision hypothesis is to be accepted, then it is expected that the dependent variable will increase over time. Model 2 uses the same techniques. A form of the Capital Asset Pricing Model replaces the regression specification used in Model 1. In addition, both models were re-estimated using dummy variables to indicate the presence of an M-form organization.

The results from the models and their variations do not provide strong evidence which supports the multidivision hypothesis. For most forms of the models the number of firms increasing their profitability after the adoption of the M-form organization is approximately equal to the number of firms which had a decrease in profitability. For no model is the number of firms experiencing increasing profitability significantly different from the random result. Correlation analysis of the results from the different models shows that most of these results are highly related.

There are two trends which provide some support to the multidivision hypothesis. Many firms which were performing poorly at the time of their adoption of the M-form organization have improved their performance under the M-form. This evidence suggests that when the M-form is part of an adaptive response to poor performance, it provides the type of help contemplated in the M-form hypothesis. These firms are logical candidates for a series of case studies to see why the firms were performing poorly and if the M-form organization contributed to their improved performance.

4

The Adoption of the Multidivision
Organization: Case Studies

Previous chapters have examined statistically ways in which the multidivision organization affects behavior and performance in large corporations. These tests observed general trends among firms. The purpose of this chapter is to look closely at several firms and observe the motivations for and subsequent effects of changing their form of organization.

There are several conclusions which one can draw from these case studies. First, management is often subject to pressures that prevent it from adopting the organization form of its choice. These pressures may come from powerful people within the organization who perceive a lessening of their power in the new form of organization. These problems may be more general in that people may continue to behave under the new organization as if the old organization still existed. An $\overline{M}$-form organization often is the result. Second, even when people in the firm agree in principal that a new organization is desirable, there still is the problem of deciding what part of the firm goes into what segment of the organization. The creation of profit centers is not always a simple, straightforward process. Third, firms may need a period of adjustment before they are able to use a new organization properly. Fourth, the information necessary to classify organization forms is sometimes difficult to obtain. It may be hard to ascertain the degree of corporate control which exists. In addition, an organization which appears to be functionally organized may actually be of the M-form variety if transfer prices between units are set correctly. This is especially troublesome in vertically-integrated firms such as those in the oil and aluminum industries. This problem of classification is compounded by the nature of the data available. Annual reports, business magazines, and interviews are all subject to distortion. Distortion often occurs because people explain how the organization functions in terms of how it should function rather than how it does function. This may occur because people's memories are not perfect, or because different people use terms such as planning and control in different ways.

The five case studies were chosen from the group of firms which adopted an M-form organization between 1954 and 1972. Within this group, firms were selected in an attempt to provide interesting and diverse organizational histories. No attempt was made to select firms which would provide support for either the acceptance or rejection of the multidivisional hypothesis.

Kaiser Aluminum and Chemical Corporation

In 1957 Kaiser announced the establishment of "a new organizational structure consisting of six divisions...."[1] This new organization was of the M-form variety. Previously, Kaiser's organization resembled either a U-form or a U-H form. The corporation was divided into an operations group and a sales group. Control over both operations and sales was centralized.

Until the 1950s Kaiser was largely a company which produced and sold aluminum and aluminum products. The production of aluminum and its products is similar in form to that of petroleum and its products. There are four or five vertical production processes. Bauxite ore is mined. The bauxite is later processed into alumina (an aluminum oxide). The bauxite and alumina processes are often combined in one production complex. Alumina is then shipped to reduction plants where it is made into primary aluminum. Primary aluminum is usually rolled into mill products from which it is made into fabricated consumer products. Large producers of aluminum typically are vertically integrated from the mining of bauxite through the manufacture of fabrications.[2] Kaiser is no exception.

Until the number of Kaiser's product lines grew too large, a centralized functional organization was a natural way in which to organize the firm. The chemical division, which was organized after World War II, was considered to be an operating division of the corporation. Like the aluminum operations, all domestic chemical sales were made through the company's sales subsidiary. The sales subsidiary received products from the operating group at a price which was discounted from the product's market price. The sales subsidiary was not considered to be a profit center. Its line of reporting led directly into the corporation staff. Like the head of the operating group, the head of the sales subsidiary was a member of the top management staff of the corporation. The 1956 organization chart of Kaiser shows that the sales subsidiary was divided into a products grouping, a sales district grouping, and an industry grouping.

The line of reporting for the operations group led directly to the corporate staff. The operations unit was not considered to be a profit center. The operations group had four functional subgroupings which roughly corresponded to the vertical levels of aluminum production. They were raw materials operations, reduction operations, rolled products operations, and RBW (Rod, Bar, and Wire), extrusions, and forgings operations.

By 1957 the number of product lines had proliferated. Authority within the corporation was not well defined. Lines of command were part of a complex maze which included production, sales, and central purchasing. During a year of rising sales in 1956, Kaiser saw its profits drop substantially. While some of the problem was attributed to overcapacity in the aluminum industry, much was attributed to organizational problems.

Kaiser's answer to these problems was to change its organization to a multidivisional structure during 1957. Five major operating companies were formed. These companies were each established as a profit center with day-to-day operational responsibility for its broadly-defined product lines. The companies were further divided into divisions, which were often profit centers themselves. Each of the corporation's profit centers, with the exception of the Metals Division,[3] had its own sales, production, and staff organizations. In addition to the Metals Division, the companies were the Chemical Company, the Refractories Company, the Aluminum Fabricating Divisions, and the International Company.

The corporate staff was given the responsibility of control and coordination of the operations of the operating companies. Kaiser characterized the types of controls used to assure good divisional performance as being of the customary type used in many American corporations.[4] These included an annual profit plan and operating budget, cost reduction programs, and capital budgets. The performances of the operating companies were evaluated against their plans.

It is interesting to observe that during the 1960s Kaiser grew at a fast pace. The new organization form contributed to this growth. Freedom from operational responsibilities gave top management the opportunity to concentrate on long-term considerations. As a result the chemical company developed into a large U.S. company, with international operations in fourteen countries by 1962.

Product lines and market areas were not the only growth commodities during the 1960s. The number of corporate executives also grew. As a result, responsibility for coordination and control at the top became fragmented. A particularly troublesome problem was the establishment of transfer prices between profit centers. This was a particularly important issue because of both the large degree of vertical integration and the absence of markets for some of the intermediate products. In 1973, the organization of the corporate office was simplified. Instead of reporting through any of several vice presidents, both operating managers and staff specialists now reported to the president and chief executive officer. As a result, internal disputes were more easily settled within the M-form organization.

H.J. Heinz Company

The H.J. Heinz Company has primarily been engaged in the processing, packing, and selling of food products. While it is still largely in these businesses, since the mid-1960s Heinz has made a strong effort to diversify. The first corporate decision to pursue acquisitions was made in 1958. The subsequent search for companies to acquire was limited to those which were engaged in food processing. As a result of this quest, Heinz acquired Star-Kist and Ore-Ida in the United States and Plasmon in Italy. In 1966, R. Burt Gookin, Heinz's President and Chief Executive spoke about the effect of these acquisitions on Heinz's organization:

> Recognizing that our acquisitions since 1958 have made Heinz a vastly different company, we have been reorganizing our executive team at corporate headquarters. One of our principal goals is simply to develop and expand our new subsidiaries that we plan to add. We have placed prime responsibility for improved sales and earnings more directly with the managers of each affiliate, and at the same time created new posts charged with developing ways to improve profitability and to better coordinate the operations of all affiliates. [5]

The reorganization that occurred in 1966 eventually changed Heinz from a firm with a U-H form of organization to one with an M-form. Prior to the 1966 reorganization, Heinz's United States operating division was organized along functional lines. Executives in the United States operating company also served as corporate executives. The international operations all reported through an executive vice president. Corporate control over the international affiliates was primarily financial and was loose and limited. The affiliates did their own long-term planning and also raised their own capital.

The 1957 organization, which is described in great detail in a case study by the Controllership Foundation,[6] continued to exist in much the same form until the 1966 reorganization. This organization had been in existence since at least 1935. In 1957, besides its domestic operations, Heinz had three foreign subsidiaries. They were located in England, Australia, and Canada. They became part of Heinz in 1917, 1935, and 1940 respectively. Until the 1966 reorganization, all of Heinz's foreign subsidiaries had a great deal of independence. The companies were staffed and managed by local people whose job was to direct themselves to the local market in which they worked. Marketing, product selection, recipes, and packing were all local decisions. Each of Heinz's operating divisions was organized functionally.

As in most corporations, the nominal responsibility for long-term formulation of policy and for performance is with the Board of Directors and its executive committee. In Heinz the executive committee played a relatively active role in the pre-1966 organization. It formulated basic policy objectives and reviewed the performance of the operating companies. Still, this participation was limited to annual reviews. Most of the power to formulate budgets and evaluate performance was in the individual companies.

Because of its dual role as corporate staff and operating company, the United States company's operating units were particularly important. The United States company was organized into seven functional units which reported to the Vice President of United States Operations. These units, which were called divisions, included units with responsibility for manufacturing, purchasing, research and quality control, the comptroller's functions, purchasing, marketing, sales, and transportation. The heads of these divisions made up the Operating Committee. The Operating Committee had primary overview responsibility. The Vice President of United States Operations, like counterparts in the foreign subsidiaries, had profit responsibility.

Day-to-day responsibility varied from function to function. Manufacturing responsibility was rather decentralized, as was marketing. In both cases, most primary responsibility rested in the functional department. Pricing, on the other hand, was the responsibility of both the marketing department and the comptroller. In the event of disputes, the Vice President of United States Operations had final authority.

The Comptroller's division had the greatest responsibility for control and coordination. It put together profit and cash plans and evaluated results based on these plans. The operating divisions each provided the segment of the plan, and the information relevant to it, for which they were most closely involved. The Comptroller's division reviewed these plans for accuracy, internal consistency, and compatibility with overall corporate goals. Problems were solved through discussions between the Comptroller's division and the relevant divisions. The Comptroller's division used a standardized cost accounting system, from which they helped to evaluate the performance of the functional divisions. This was facilitated by having members of the Comptroller's division working in the functional divisions.

There were two operating plans formulated by the Controller's division. One was an annual plan, the other was a five-year plan. In addition to these two plans, a capital budget was developed. Within this budget each capital expenditure was evaluated based on necessity, growth and profit potential, timing, and amount of request.

To summarize, previous to the 1966 reorganization Heinz was organized as a U-H form firm. Domestic operations were functionally organized with day-to-day operational control in the functional departments. Planning, coordination, and control were nominally corporate responsibilities with actual responsibility in the Comptroller's division. The foreign subsidiaries were quite independent with the corporate staff providing little control or guidance.

By 1966, Heinz was manufacturing products in thirteen countries and territories and selling them in 150. As a result, management decided that a new corporate organization was needed. A world corporate headquarters was established, with responsibility for long-term planning, coordination, and control. Planning and review have each been handled through a separate annual process. The intent of the Heinz organization was to place operating responsibility as far down into the organization as possible. The manager of each operating unit has ultimate responsibility for maximizing financial return. Growth is also a major corporate goal.

Unlike many corporations which have divisionalized, Heinz established most of its operating units along geographic instead of product lines. The exceptions are the Ore-Ida and Sun-Kist divisions.

The divisionalized organization adopted in 1966 has been refined since then. It is not clear to what extent the extensive budgeting systems employed by Heinz allow the corporate staff to perform properly the functions of coordination and control over the operating divisions. The infrastructure which exists is that of an M-form organization, and for this reason Heinz has been so classified. However, if effective coordination and control are not performed by the corporate staff, a more suitable classification would be that of H-form.

Burlington Industries, Inc.

Burlington Industries was founded in 1923 by James S. Love. By the time of his death in 1962, Love had transformed Burlington Industries from a small cotton mill to a complex billion dollar textile company. Since 1962, Love's successors have slowed his active acquisition policy. Still, the size of the firm has doubled, mostly through internal growth. During Love's lifetime, Burlington had various hybrid organizations which used different degrees of decentralization. E.J. Mack of Burlington feels that a division's decentralization was determined by numerous factors including its interdependence with other Burlington divisions, the manner in which the division was acquired, and the personalities involved.[7]

In the 1950s several attempts were made to rationalize Burlington's organization. Before these attempts, Burlington was a sprawling company with little organizational form. There were some divisions which were rather independent and which handled their own manufacturing, merchandising, and, to some degree, administration. Typically, though, merchandising groups operated independently from manufacturing groups. There also existed a group of plants which either sold their product to a group of sales divisions or sold their product through these divisions. Presumably, there was some form of transfer mechanism related to either cost or price. Love tried to keep track of the operating units through memoranda and face-to-face meetings with operating personnel. There is little indication that Burlington had either a systematic method of gathering data on the performance of operating units or a systematic method of allocating capital to these units. The primary method of control seems to have been through the large amount of personal loyalty which existed between Love and the heads of the operating units, many of whom were trained and placed in their positions by Love. Until the 1950s, though, the controller's function was centralized, after which it became more independent. Either a U-H or H-form classification seems appropriate for this period.

During the 1950s Burlington grew at a tremendously quick rate, mostly through acquisitions. In 1953, the need for a rationalization of the organizational structure became apparent, and Burlington announced a consolidation and decentralization of its operating units.

> Working under the top officials of Burlington Mills are division managers, heading up manufacturing and selling areas grouped by products and their end uses. Services are broken down into departments with department heads. Under the division managers are group managers who direct specialized operations in production or marketing.[8]

> During the year, increased emphasis was placed on decentralization of authority and responsibility for subsidiary operations.... These Divisions integrate both selling and manufacturing responsibilities and achieve a more efficient overall operation.[9]

In 1954 there were seven domestic divisions and an international division. By 1962, this had increased to thirty-six divisions. Each division was organized as a profit center, was run by its own president, and had its own sales and manufacturing units. Some of these divisions were suppliers to other divisions and were required to transfer their products at cost to other Burlington divisions. Because there is no indication of the appropriate corporate controls, a H-form classification seems most likely, though an M'-form would not be inappropriate.

After Love's death, the new management felt that it was necessary to gain some control over the operating divisions. These divisions had been largely autonomous. The new management kept the divisions as independent profit centers. The divisions were then grouped according to market segment. Increased controls were placed on the operations of the divisions. Divisions were required to submit proposals for capital spending to top management for approval. The 1969 annual report describes the overall organization and control apparatus.

> Burlington Industries has 31 operating divisions each with its own market, its own sales, and manufacturing management. Each division president is an experienced executive, close to his division's markets and able to react quickly to new trends or changes. He has the responsibility and authority to make adjustments in product, price, production levels or other factors affecting his business.
> Operations are audited, and evaluated, with return on investment the basic yardstick. Compensation and new investment decisions are related to results. Corporate management,

recently reorganized to provide a more streamlined approach to the management demands of the Seventies, has these primary functions:

1. Establish broad corporate policy,
2. Plan and evaluate capital expenditures,
3. Develop managers and plan the organizational structure,
4. Plan new directions for future business opportunities.[10]

It seems that these controls have been evolving since at least 1962, though the exact date they were fully effective is not known. For lack of better information, a starting date of 1962 is assigned.

Like IBM, Burlington Industries is interesting to study because of its unusual organizational history. Its early organization was a hybrid of a functional organization and a decentralized organization with loose controls. This hybrid organization apparently resulted from the combination of the one-person rule of James Love and the rapid acquisition process which Burlington experienced. While consolidation and rationalization of the organization were tried by Burlington starting in 1953, a true M-form organization did not exist until after Love's death. This type of problem is not uncommon. Even when the founder of a company agrees that change is desired, the changes necessary to achieve a true M-form organization often run counter to the way the founder has been running the business. While the organizations which existed prior to their adoptions of the M-form differ, the experiences of Burlington and IBM in this regard were quite similar and typical.

International Business Machine Corporation

The International Business Machine Corporation is now, and has been for some time, the world's dominant producer and seller of data processing equipment. While virtually all of IBM's business is in the computer and related fields, the differences between products in these fields and differences between the markets in which they are sold make IBM a complex diversified company for purposes of reviewing its organization.

The company was the product of Thomas Watson, Sr. who ran the company until 1956 when he was replaced by his son, Thomas Watson, Jr. Prior to 1956, IBM used a highly centralized functional organization. The senior Watson personally kept track of all segments of the company. In the late 1940s, before he delegated some authority to his sons, Watson had thirty-five lines from management reporting to him. The pre-1956 organization is described by T.M. Liptak of IBM:

> IBM was a functional organization; both line functions (engineering, manufacturing, sales, etc.) and the few existing staff functions (legal, personnel, budgets, etc.) reported to the IBM President. There were no divisions, no profit centers below the Corporation, and no formal

staff. Day-to-day operations responsibility resided with the line function heads (e.g. sales, engineering, etc.) subject to existing corporate controls.[11]

That the highly centralized decision-making process left IBM's top management with little time for long-term strategic planning is illustrated by two missed strategic opportunities. The first occurred in the late 1940s when IBM failed to take advantage of an opportunity to purchase Eckert-Mauchly, a pioneer in computer design. Instead Eckert-Mauchly was purchased by Remington Rand who later became a leader in early computer technology. Until it observed Remington Rand's success, IBM was content to continue to produce and sell data processing equipment which utilized the older electro-mechanical process. The second missed opportunity occurred in the 1950s. IBM decided not to acquire the rights to the xerographic copier developed by Haloid Xerox, Inc. Thomas Watson, Jr. felt these missed opportunities were the result of complacency among IBM people.[12] More than likely they were the result of the lack of time available to top management under the centralized functional organization.

In 1956, IBM signed a consent decree which terminated a Justice Department action against it. Thomas Watson, Sr. opposed the signing of the decree. Soon after the signing of the decree he resigned. Thomas Watson, Jr. assumed full command of the corporation.

> The timing was fortunate. The elder Watson had carried the company to what may have been its maximum size under centralized, monolithic management. It needed new blood to reorganize it for handling the even bigger jobs then pressing.[13]

The task of reorganizing IBM was a massive one. Watson observed that while IBM had a fine sales organization, it was deficient in almost all other areas of management. As a result when IBM decided to divisionalize in 1956, many executives were placed in positions for which they were not prepared. Many people who had previously held operating positions were in staff positions under the new organization. While this often occurs in firms as they adopt an M-form organization, the problem seems to have been particularly acute at IBM. This may account for the subsequent problems IBM has had in organizing its Data Processing Division.

The 1956 reorganization produced one large division and four smaller divisions. The large division was the Data Processing Division. The smaller divisions were the Federal Systems Division, the Electric Typewriter Division, the Time Equipment Division, and the Service Bureau Corporation. The divisions were autonomous profit centers, each with its own manufacturing, research, and sales departments. The corporate staff, which had a great deal of power, had the responsibility of transmitting corporate policy and of advising operational management. The Corporate Management Committee, headed by

Watson, settled disputes between line and staff personnel. Since 1956, the corporation's executive staff has had the responsibility of establishing IBM's basic policies, approving the plans of the divisions, and appraising performance throughout the firm.

While IBM had successfully organized itself into an M-form firm with autonomous profit centers and the requisite controls, several problems remained. For one, the number of management levels between top management and operating management was still large. Nine levels existed in production and eight in sales. The second problem involved the handling of the Data Processing Division, which accounted for approximately 80% of the company's sales. After groping with this problem the decision was made to divide this division into three autonomous manufacturing units and one independent sales unit. The three manufacturing units were concerned with large computer systems, small computer systems, and new product development.

IBM has retained the same basic organization form since 1956. Divisions have remained autonomous profit centers with responsibility for planning and control being retained by the corporate staff. The data processing part of the business, however, has been reorganized. Because the two computer manufacturing divisions established in 1958 eventually began to compete with each other, they were combined along with the other data processing units into the DP Group in 1966. Responsibilities which had been given to the manufacturing and sales division under the old organization now were given to the DP Group.

> The DP Group established in 1966, was designated a single profit center. The change meant increased delegation of authority to the Group for operational matters, while planning and control responsibility was retained at corporate headquarters.[14]

The DP Group was organized into four U.S. geographic regions and thirteen specialized industry sections. The geographic regions were considered to be profit centers.

Except for the size of the data processing unit, its internal organization would not be of interest in evaluating IBM's organizational form. Because data processing accounts for such a large part of IBM's sales and because it has usually had a functional organization, there is a temptation to assign to IBM either a U-H form or X-form organization. However, if data processing is subject to large economies of scale (which seems to be the case), if operating and strategic decisions are properly separated, and if the corporate staff retains the proper tools for planning, control and coordination, then an M-form classification is the correct assignment. Since this seems to have been the case for IBM, it is felt that its organization is M-form. Because there is some indication that members of the corporate staff were overly concerned with operational responsibility in the data processing units, it is possible that for 1959-66 an $\overline{M}$-form classification is proper.

In 1972, IBM broke up the DP Group and established an organization similar to that which existed prior to 1966. This organization has been retained at least through 1974. Four group vice-presidents were each given operational responsibility over several "divisions." These four have reported directly to the top corporate staff. The data processing "divisions" are not profit centers, but rather reflect a division between sales and production. Data processing sales is located in a different group from data processing manufacturing and development. A classification of either a U-H form or a X-form may be appropriate.

Studying IBM's organizational history provides interesting insights into both the difficulties experienced in adopting a new organization and the difficulties inherent in classifying these organizations. It is possible that IBM should not have adopted an M-form organization in 1956. Because of the relative size of the data processing units, an X-form organization may have been more appropriate. This would have placed top management in charge of a relatively homogenous business. This is the classic U-form environment. If the non-data processing divisions had M-form type controls, the organization would be of the X-form type. Actually, IBM may have had such an organization since 1972. On the other hand, an X-form organization for a division the size of data processing may strain the capacity of top management. If this were the case for IBM, then the usual reasons for preferring an M-form organization would still hold.

Honeywell, Inc.

Honeywell was founded in 1927 as a result of a merger between the Heating Specialties Company and the Minneapolis Heat Regulator Company. Prior to World War II it manufactured and sold a wide variety of temperature controlling and heat regulatory devices. With the advent of World War II, Honeywell expanded into new control-related areas including the production of automatic pilots for aircraft. After the war, Honeywell elected to remain in the business of producing military equipment. In 1955 the company further expanded its product base by entering the electronic data processing field through the formation of Datamatic Corporation. Datamatic was initially a partnership with Raytheon. In 1957 Raytheon sold its share to Honeywell.

By slowly entering new product areas which were extensions of its existing product mix, Honeywell grew from a small relatively homogenous company to one which is now large and diverse. As the character of the company's sales changed, so did its form of organization. Paul R. Elsen of Honeywell notes:

> Prior to 1941 Honeywell was centrally controlled and functionally organized except for the Brown Instrument Division, which was operated as a separate profit center. The subsidiaries were directed quite centrally via operations plans, performance reporting and central product development.[15]

The subsidiaries mentioned include the Brown Instrument Division which was a wholly-owned subsidiary which manufactured and sold various indicating, recording, and controlling instruments which were used in industrial processes. The other subsidiaries were foreign operations of Honeywell in Canada, England, and Sweden.

Previous to its entry into the sale of military equipment. Honeywell was a company with one basic product line. Like most companies with a large degree of product homogeneity, Honeywell used a centralized functional organization. Over the years, though, Honeywell retained an organization with tight centralized control of day-to-day functional operations. This can be attributed to two main factors. First, though Honeywell expanded into new product fields, these fields were to a large degree extensions of existing fields. Second, Honeywell was run by Harold W. Sweatt from 1934 through 1961. Sweatt felt strongly that Honeywell should avoid the trappings of a large firm. As a result he attempted to keep controls centralized, with responsibilities and authority channeled into himself. So, when Honeywell introduced a divisionalized organization in 1941 it was of the M-form variety. Mr. Elsen describes it:

> During the years from 1941 to 1961 a semi-decentralized operating method was used by Harold Sweatt. Although divisions were set up, they in fact were incomplete entities in most cases. Sales and manufacturing, for example, were quite centralized. The corporate staff entered into a wide variety of issues at all levels of the organization. There was an attempt to summarize the division's [sic] performance as separate profit centers, but in practice this proved to be a very difficult accounting task.[16]

Mr. Elsen notes that Jim Binger, Honeywell's Chairman of the Board and the person who eventually introduced an M-form organization to Honeywell, feels that the organization from 1941 through 1961 worked well. According to Mr. Binger, Honeywell was not ready for a fully decentralized organization in terms of available management, geographic dispersion, and market penetration.

In 1961, Binger became Honeywell's President. Almost immediately, Honeywell adopted a fully decentralized organization, though it did take a few years for the new profit center to be formed properly. The new organization attempted to keep top management at a minimum, with the focus of both operational and planning decisions being made at the divisional level. The divisions are monitored through a series of meetings with Honeywell's Executive Committee. Each division presents its plans for sales, profits, return on investment, and capital requirements for the coming year. After negotiations, a plan is formulated and the division is free to operate. A midyear review includes plans for the ensuing four year period.

Since 1961, Honeywell has continued to specialize in four broad product areas. They are control systems for homes and buildings, control systems for industry, control systems for aerospace and defense, and information systems. Divisions are placed into groups according to the division's major product line.

While the divisions are independent profit centers, they are subject to a variety of controls from the corporate staff. A division's performance is evaluated against the profit, sales, and rate of return goals outlined in its annual plan. In addition, capital is allocated among divisions according to the rate of return on the capital and the riskiness of the project. The performance of the division is monitored throughout the year by the central staff through data received from the divisions. These controls are typical of those found in M-form organizations.

5

Conclusions

The purpose of this analysis has been to examine some of the ways in which the performance of large corporations is affected by their choice of organizational form. The study has been motivated by the work of Alfred D. Chandler and Oliver E. Williamson. After examining histories of numerous major American corporations, Chandler concluded that the formation of a multidivisional (M-form) organization has been an important adaptive response used by corporations to correct inefficiencies resulting from increased size and diversity. Williamson, drawing heavily from the literature on organization theory, came to the same conclusion. As a result of his work, Williamson proposed the multidivision form hypothesis, which states:

> ...the organization and operation of the large enterprise along the lines of the M-form favors goal-pursuit and least-cost behavior more nearly associated with the neo-classical profit-maximization hypothesis than does the U-form organizational alternative[1]

In the present study, the M-form hypothesis and its consequences are examined in three different ways. First, the effect of organization form on the level of executive compensation is examined. Second, the M-form hypothesis is tested directly. The effect of the adoption of the M-form organization on the profitability of firms is examined. Finally, case studies of five firms which adopted the M-form organization are constructed and analyzed.

The results of these individual studies are mixed. While some evidence can be found in them which supports the M-form hypothesis, the results are far from conclusive. Chapter 2 examined the compensation packages of U-form and M-form firms. The results from the zero-tests show that after accounting for the effects of sales, profitability, and selling and administative expense M-form firms have higher levels of executive compensation than do U-form firms. This is seen as being consistent with the hierarchial model proposed by Herbert Simon. A second series of tests drops the assumption of equal elasticities of compensation with respect to sales, profitability, and selling and administrative expense in U-form and M-form firms. The elasticities with respect to profitability are found to be equal for U-form and M-form firms. M-form firms, however, show higher elasticities with respect to sales do than U-form firms. In addition, M-form firms penalize staff expansion bias to a greater degree than do U-form firms. It is concluded that the compensation packages of the M-form firms are more like those of a long-run profit-maximizing firm than are those of U-form firms.

Chapter 3 provides a direct test of the multidivisional hypothesis. The effect of the adoption of the M-form organization on the profitability of sample firms is tested. Two models and their variations are used. No differential effect on profitability caused by organization form is shown. Two patterns are found which may be indicative of the positive effect the M-form organization has on profitability. Firms adopting the M-form organization in the latter part of the sample improved their performance under the M-form organization to a greater degree than did firms adopting the M-form organization during the earlier years. This pattern is consistent with both the notion that an organizational innovation requires a period of learning before it is able to work to its potential and that firms learn by observing the experiences of others. The second pattern showed that among those firms with below average profitability in the year the M-form organization was adopted, a large majority improved their performance during the test period. Since the M-form organization is viewed as an adaptive response to a decline in corporate performance, it is firms with subpar profitability in the year of adoption which are most expected to benefit from the adoption of the M-form organization.

Several problems inherent in the profitability analysis bias its results towards rejecting the multidivisional hypothesis. The two most important reasons involve the timing of the adoption of the M-form organization. First, the analysis assumes that firms operate the M-form organization only after performing poorly under the U-form organization for a period of time. If the M-form organization is adopted at the optimal moment, no differential in profitability will be detected even if the M-form hypothesis is correct. Second, if firms adopt the M-form organization prematurely, the analysis will tend to reject the M-form hypothesis since the set of M-form firms will include firms who should not be so organized. The superior improvement of firms with subpar profitability in the year the M-form was adopted provides some support for the notion that the analysis is subject to these problems.

The case studies described in chapter 4 provide additional insight into the reasons why the analyses do not provide strong support for the M-form hypothesis. On the operational side, the formation of an M-form organization is often not easy. Pressures within the old organization from people who perceive a loss of power under the new organization may cause some problems. In addition, the creation of profit centers and their placement within the overall organization is not always a simple process. Finally, even when a structurally sound M-form organization is established, the people within it need time to learn how to behave properly. This learning time may differ from firm to firm.

On the classification side, the assignment of the various organizational forms to firms is subject to a great deal of measurement error. While the definitions of the various organization forms produce a neat taxonomy, many firms do not fall easily into one particular category. In addition, data on a firm's organizational history are often difficult to obtain. These problems are particularly acute when dealing with vertically integrated firms. The correct assignment of an M-form classification depends on knowledge of the firm's transfer pricing methods. This knowledge is difficult to obtain and, when obtained, difficult to interpret.

While these analyses do not provide strong evidence in support of the M-form hypothesis, they do provide some insight both into the ways in which M-form firms operate and into ways in which this behavior can be statistically modeled. The work by Chandler and Williamson give compelling testimony in support of the M-form hypothesis. The analyses undertaken in this study show that organizational form affects behavior. It also provides some evidence in support of the M-form hypothesis. Because of the importance of the M-form innovation, both in terms of potential effect within a firm and in the extent of diffusion across firms, further statistical work along the lines developed in this study with refined data seems warranted.

Appendix A

Executive Compensation Data and Variable Definitions

Data Definitions:

Position:

Executive compensation data were collected for the chief executive officer in each of the companies in the sample. The title of the chief executive officer varied from company to company. For most of the companies in the sample, the position of chief executive officer carried the title of President, with the title of Chairman of the Board connoting an honorary position.

Common Shares:

Proxy reports were consulted for the stock holdings of the chief executives. In those cases where the proxy reports did not contain the needed information, the SEC publication *Official Summary of Security Transactions and Holdings* was consulted. Data on stock holdings included those shares that were either directly or beneficially owned by the chief executive or by his immediate family. "An example of beneficial ownership as interpreted by the SEC, would be a situation in which shares are temporarily held in trust for the man in question under an arrangement calling for his receipt of the annual dividends thereon and for the subsequent distribution of the shares to him upon, say, the demise of a relative. Alternatively, the securities might be nominally owned by a private holding company, which in turn would be controlled by the man and his family. In either case, the pecuniary rewards and contingencies of a direct ownership position are effectively transmitted to the individual executive, and the shares at issue properly considered part of his total portfolio."[1]

Current Remuneration:

Proxy statements were consulted. In those cases where the proxy reports did not contain the needed information, *Business Week's* "Annual Survey of Executive Compensation" was consulted. Current remuneration includes direct salary and any bonuses received by the executive.

Deferred Remuneration:

Proxy statements were consulted. In those cases where the proxy reports did not contain the needed information, *Business Week's* "Annual Survey of Executive Compensation" was consulted. Deferred Remuneration includes both money and stock payments. The value of the deferred remuneration was determined by finding the present value of the deferred remuneration for the year in which it was issued. A 6% rate of interest was used.[2] It was assumed that all executives still employed in 1973 would retire in 1978.

Retirement Income:

Proxy statements were consulted. No other source of data is available. When an observation was missing, it was assigned the mean value of the observations of the years immediately before and after the year in question. Because the value of retirement income rarely changes quickly for a given executive, this procedure caused little loss in accuracy. The value of retirement income was determined by taking the rate charged by New England Mutual (Life) Insurance Company for a 55 year old male for a retirement income policy effective at age 65.

Stock Options:

Proxy reports were consulted. Backup sources were both the *Business Week* "Annual Survey of Executive Compensation" and the SEC publication *Official Summary of Security Transactions and Holdings.* For those options already exercised, the worth of the option was determined by taking the differences between the option and the market prices on the day the option was exercised. For options still outstanding in 1973, two assumptions were tried in an effort to value the options. The first assumption was that if an option were not exercised by December 31, 1973, it was not exercised. The second assumption was that if an option were not exercised by December 31, 1973 and the option price was less than the closing market price on this date, the option was exercised on December 31, 1973. Once the worth of the option was ascertained, the value was defined as the discounted stream of the value of the stock option. A 6% rate of discount was assumed.

Dividend Income:

Dividend income was determined by multiplying the dividend per share of common stock by the number of shares of common stock listed under *common shares.* Dividend per share data was available on the Standard and Poor's *Compustat Tape* for 1952-1970. For other years the data was found in the company's annual report.

Tax Liabilities

All forms of executive compensation were valued at their after tax level. It was assumed that an executive earned an additional income equal to 10% of salary plus dividends. The average tax liability was found by consulting the IRS publication *Statistics of Income.* To find the average tax liability for income earned after retirement, it was assumed that the executive would be earning between $100,000 and $150,000 per year. The tax rate for stock options and capital gains was set at 15%.

Capital Gains

Capital Gains were calculated by adding together "paper" gains with realized gains. In each case, the stock was valued on December 31. Paper gains were calculated by taking the change in price over the year and multiplying it by the number of shares held for the full year. For a change in number of shares held, it was assumed that the transaction occurred at a price midway between the prices at the start and end of the year.

Variable Definitions:

REMUN:

This definition of compensation includes only current remuneration (Salary + bonus).

TREM:

TREM = REMUN + deferred remuneration + retirement income.

COMPN:

COMPN = TREM + value of stock options (options outstanding on December 31, 1973, are assumed to have been not exercised).

CMPN:

CMPN = TREM + value of stock options (options outstanding on December 31, 1973, are assumed to be exercised on December 31, 1973 if the option price is less than the market price).

Equation 2-3

$$\log(EC)_{it} = d_0 + d_1\log(SALESU)_{it-1} + d_2\log(SALESM)_{it-1} + d_3\log(RRU)_{it-1} + d_4\log(RRM)_{it-1} + d_5 Years_{it}$$

Equation 2-3

Compensation Definition: REMUN
Profitability Definition: Rate of Return on Assets

d_0 = 4.875
d_1 = 0.066   (4.08)
d_2 = 0.106   (6.71)
d_3 = 0.295   (7.49)
d_4 = 0.243   (5.53)
d_5 = 0.003   (2.39)

R^2 = .36 $F(5, 393)$ = 44.82

t-statistics are in parentheses

Equation 2-3

Compensation Definition: TREM
Profitability Definition: Rate of Return on Assets

d_0 = 4.901
d_1 = 0.086   (5.31)
d_2 = 0.147   (9.20)
d_3 = 0.328   (8.26)
d_4 = 0.325   (7.35)
d_5 = 0.002   (1.23)

$R^2 = .41$ $F(5, 393) = 55.42$

t-statistics are in parentheses

Equation 2-3

Compensation Definition: COMPN
Profitability Definition: Rate of Return on Assets

d_0 =   4.948
d_1 =   0.161   (8.00)
d_2 =   0.203   (10.21)
d_3 =   0.490   (9.91)
d_4 =   0.474   (8.62)
d_5 =   -0.002   (-1.01)

$R^2 = .39$ $F(5, 393) = 51.07$

t-statistics are in parentheses

Equation 2-3

Compensation Definition: CMPN
Profitability Definition: Rate of Return on Assets

d_0 =   4.950
d_1 =   0.167   (7.44)
d_2 =   0.216   (9.74)
d_3 =   0.502   (9.09)
d_4 =   0.493   (8.04)
d_5 =   -0.002   (-0.93)

$R^2 = .36$ $F(5, 393) = 45.23$

t-statistics are in parentheses

Equation 2-3

Compensation Definition: REMUN
Profitability Definition: Rate of Return on Equity

d_0 =   4.886
d_1 =   0.156   (7.99)
d_2 =   0.133   (9.72)
d_3 =   0.560   (10.87)
d_4 =   0.340   (8.93)
d_5 =   0.004   (2.84)

$R^2 = .48$ $F(5, 393) = 73.19$

t-statistics are in parentheses

Equation 2-3

Compensation Definition: TREM
Profitability Definition: Rate of Return on Equity

d_0 = 4.913
d_1 = 0.176 (8.97)
d_2 = 0.169 (12.31)
d_3 = 0.592 (11.44)
d_4 = 0.411 (10.74)
d_5 = 0.002 (1.57)

R^2 = .52 $F(5, 393)$ = 87.34

t-statistics are in parentheses

Equation 2-3

Compensation Definition: COMPN
Profitability Definition: Rate of Return on Equity

d_0 = 4.960
d_1 = 0.272 (10.75)
d_2 = 0.211 (11.90)
d_3 = 0.812 (12.17)
d_4 = 0.519 (10.52)
d_5 = -0.001 (-0.89)

R^2 = .47 $F(5, 393)$ = 70.58

t-statistics are in parentheses

Equation 2-3

Compensation Definition: CMPN
Profitability Definition: Rate of Return on Equity

d_0 = 4.962
d_1 = 0.280 (9.80)
d_2 = 0.227 (11.33)
d_3 = 0.827 (11.00)
d_4 = 0.546 (9.81)
d_5 = -0.002 (-0.82)

R^2 = .43 $F(5, 393)$ = 61.09

t-statistics are in parentheses

Equation 2-4

$$\log(EC)_{it} = e_0 + e_1\log(SALESU)_{it-1} + e_2\log(SALESM)_{it-1}$$
$$+ e_3\log(RRU)_{it-1} + e_4\log(RRM)_{it-1} + e_5\log(PSell\ U)_{it-1}$$
$$+ e_6\log(PSell\ M)_{it-1} + e_7 Years_{it}$$

Equation 2-4

Compensation Definition: COMPN
Profitability Definition: Rate of Return on Assets

$$
\begin{aligned}
e_0 &= 4.877 \\
e_1 &= 0.054 & (\ 2.62) \\
e_2 &= 0.153 & (\ 5.29) \\
e_3 &= 0.292 & (\ 7.38) \\
e_4 &= 0.252 & (\ 5.72) \\
e_5 &= 0.013 & (\ 0.82) \\
e_6 &= -0.058 & (-1.92) \\
e_7 &= 0.003 & (\ 2.20)
\end{aligned}
$$

$R^2 = .36$ $F(7, 391) = 32.84$

t-statistics are in parentheses

Equation 2-4

Compensation Definition: TREM
Profitability Definition: Rate of Return on Assets

$$
\begin{aligned}
e_0 &= 4.905 \\
e_1 &= 0.079 & (\ 3.81) \\
e_2 &= 0.203 & (\ 6.97) \\
e_3 &= 0.326 & (\ 8.20) \\
e_4 &= 0.337 & (\ 7.60) \\
e_5 &= 0.007 & (\ 0.45) \\
e_6 &= -0.071 & (-2.30) \\
e_7 &= 0.001 & (\ 0.98)
\end{aligned}
$$

$R^2 = .41$ $F(7, 391) = 40.73$

t-statistics are in parentheses

Equation 2-4

Compensation Definition: COMPN
Profitability Definition: Rate of Return on Assets

$$
\begin{aligned}
e_0 &= 4.943 \\
e_1 &= 0.135 & (\ 5.22) \\
e_2 &= 0.202 & (\ 5.57) \\
e_3 &= 0.482 & (\ 9.71) \\
e_4 &= 0.473 & (\ 8.55) \\
e_5 &= 0.031 & (\ 1.56) \\
e_6 &= 0.001 & (\ 0.03) \\
e_7 &= -0.002 & (-0.83)
\end{aligned}
$$

$R^2 = .39$ $F(7, 391) = 36.87$

t-statistics are in parentheses

Equation 2-4

Compensation Definition: CMPN
Profitability Definition: Rate of Return on Assets

$$e_0 = 4.942$$
$$e_1 = 0.139 \quad (4.82)$$
$$e_2 = 0.197 \quad (4.85)$$
$$e_3 = 0.493 \quad (8.89)$$
$$e_4 = 0.488 \quad (7.90)$$
$$e_5 = 0.034 \quad (1.55)$$
$$e_6 = 0.025 \quad (0.57)$$
$$e_7 = -0.001 \quad (-0.70)$$

$R^2 = .36 \quad F(7, 391) = 32.75$

t-statistics are in parentheses

Equation 2-4

Compensation Definition: REMUN
Profitability Definition: Rate of Return on Equity

$$e_0 = 4.889$$
$$e_1 = 0.156 \quad (6.56)$$
$$e_2 = 0.162 \quad (6.60)$$
$$e_3 = 0.560 \quad (10.73)$$
$$e_4 = 0.340 \quad (8.93)$$
$$e_5 = -0.0004 \quad (-0.03)$$
$$e_6 = -0.039 \quad (-1.25)$$
$$e_7 = 0.003 \quad (2.63)$$

$R^2 = .48 \quad F(7, 391) = 52.58$

t-statistics are in parentheses

Equation 2-4

Compensation Definition: TREM
Profitability Definition: Rate of Return on Equity

$$e_0 = 4.917$$
$$e_1 = 0.181 \quad (7.61)$$
$$e_2 = 0.202 \quad (8.20)$$
$$e_3 = 0.595 \quad (11.37)$$
$$e_4 = 0.411 \quad (10.76)$$
$$e_5 = -0.006 \quad (-0.43)$$
$$e_6 = -0.045 \quad (-1.63)$$
$$e_7 = 0.002 \quad (1.32)$$

$R^2 = .52 \quad F(7, 391) = 62.92$

t-statistics are in parentheses

Equation 2-4

Compensation Definition: COMPN
Profitability Definition: Rate of Return on Equity

$$
\begin{aligned}
e_0 &= 4.955 \\
e_1 &= 0.259 & (\ 8.40) \\
e_2 &= 0.184 & (\ 5.76) \\
e_3 &= 0.804 & (\ 11.89) \\
e_4 &= 0.518 & (\ 10.50) \\
e_5 &= 0.015 & (\ 0.79) \\
e_6 &= 0.038 & (\ 1.06) \\
e_7 &= -0.001 & (-0.67)
\end{aligned}
$$

$R^2 = .47$ $F(7, 391) = 50.62$

t-statistics are in parentheses

Equation 2-4

Compensation Definition: CMPN
Profitability Definition: Rate of Return on Equity

$$
\begin{aligned}
e_0 &= 4.955 \\
e_1 &= 0.264 & (\ 7.61) \\
e_2 &= 0.181 & (\ 5.03) \\
e_3 &= 0.817 & (\ 10.74) \\
e_4 &= 0.544 & (\ 9.80) \\
e_5 &= 0.018 & (\ 0.84) \\
e_6 &= 0.063 & (\ 1.57) \\
e_7 &= -0.001 & (-0.55)
\end{aligned}
$$

$R^2 = .43$ $F(7, 391) = 44.21$

t-statistics are in parentheses

Appendix B

Regression Results

Equation 2-1

Compensation Definition: REMUN
Profitability Definition: Rate of Return on Assets

Firm (i)	b_1		b_2	
1	0.44	(7.25)	-0.01	(-0.05)
2	.47	(12.13)	.01	(0.13)
3	.51	(5.32)	.25	(0.83)
4	.46	(9.93)	-.09	(-0.62)
5	.29	(7.33)	-.80	(-6.64)
6	.36	(6.60)	-.34	(-2.79)
7	.58	(10.25)	.50	(2.45)
8	.57	(12.35)	.25	(4.19)
9	.65	(11.33)	.37	(2.98)
10	.90	(7.95)	1.64	(3.99)
11	.54	(9.43)	.02	(0.09)
12	.50	(7.61)	-.11	(-0.73)
13	.32	(8.80)	-.81	(-6.04)
14	.59	(11.20)	.32	(2.99)
15	.54	(7.76)	.09	(0.55)
16	.78	(6.98)	.74	(2.33)
17	.53	(9.74)	.09	(0.59)
18	.42	(8.79)	-.27	(-2.20)
19	.39	(6.90)	.00	(0.10)

$R^2 = .83$ $F(41, 357) = 47.20$

$b_0 = 3.58$

$b_3 = -0.12 \ (-5.34)$

$b_4 = 0.002 \ (0.11)$

$b_5 = 0.002 \ (1.61)$

t-statistics are in parentheses

Equation 2-1

Compensation Definition: TREM
Profitability Definition: Rate of Return on Assets

Firm (i)	b_1	b_2
1	0.24 (4.31)	-0.12 (-1.33)
2	.44 (11.78)	.30 (2.53)
3	.39 (4.83)	.19 (0.72)
4	.21 (3.17)	-.63 (-2.59)
5	.27 (7.70)	-.48 (-4.15)
6	.32 (5.24)	-.13 (-1.03)
7	.51 (12.75)	.45 (3.65)
8	.52 (12.98)	.45 (5.02)
9	.68 (11.96)	.73 (5.89)
10	.62 (8.62)	.99 (3.79)
11	.49 (6.60)	.28 (1.01)
12	.41 (7.24)	-.02 (-0.14)
13	.26 (7.68)	-.55 (-4.24)
14	.75 (12.65)	1.00 (8.42)
15	.53 (8.82)	.34 (2.88)
16	.59 (10.36)	.57 (3.77)
17	.70 (13.83)	1.01 (6.87)
18	.38 (11.16)	.01 (0.29)
19	.31 (5.65)	.06 (0.42)

$R^2 = .85$ $F(41, 357) = 57.94$

$b_0 = 3.89$

$b_3 = -0.06 \ (-2.88)$

$b_4 = 0.005 \ (2.48)$

$b_5 = 0.002 \ (1.94)$

t-statistics are in parentheses

Equation 2-1

Compensation Definition: COMPN
Profitability Definition: Rate of Return on Assets

Firm (i)	b_1		b_2	
1	0.22	(2.44)	-0.17	(-1.14)
2	.45	(7.47)	.31	(1.58)
3	.36	(2.73)	.05	(0.12)
4	.41	(3.73)	-.14	(-0.37)
5	.36	(6.32)	-.48	(-2.51)
6	.31	(3.13)	-.13	(-0.63)
7	.51	(7.87)	.43	(2.16)
8	.51	(7.79)	.35	(2.40)
9	.72	(7.66)	.81	(3.97)
10	.61	(5.25)	.97	(2.25)
11	.48	(3.95)	.25	(0.56)
12	.44	(4.78)	.02	(0.09)
13	.62	(11.09)	.34	(1.59)
14	.81	(8.36)	1.13	(5.78)
15	.55	(5.57)	.34	(1.78)
16	.75	(8.00)	.98	(3.91)
17	.76	(9.05)	1.10	(4.56)
18	.40	(7.16)	.02	(0.43)
19	.32	(3.51)	.07	(0.33)

R^2 = .74 $F(41, 357)$ = 28.51

b_0 = 3.88

b_3 = -0.02 (-0.74)

b_4 = 0.04 (1.11)

b_5 = 0.001 (0.38)

t-statistics are in parentheses

Equation 2-1

Compensation Definition: CMPN
Profitability Definition: Rate of Return on Assets

Firm (i)	b_1		b_2	
1	0.29	(2.83)	-0.14	(-0.89)
2	.47	(7.06)	.23	(1.09)
3	.40	(2.75)	.05	(0.10)
4	.45	(3.68)	-.19	(-0.43)
5	.38	(5.92)	-.63	(-3.03)
6	.35	(3.20)	-.17	(-0.72)
7	.54	(7.53)	.40	(1.79)
8	.55	(7.56)	.33	(2.05)
9	.98	(9.47)	1.22	(5.46)
10	.64	(4.95)	.91	(1.93)
11	.52	(3.90)	.22	(0.44)
12	.46	(4.55)	-.02	(-0.11)
13	.69	(11.21)	.33	(1.39)
14	.81	(7.56)	1.00	(4.66)
15	.56	(5.17)	.26	(1.23)
16	1.12	(10.92)	1.83	(6.64)
17	.85	(9.20)	1.21	(4.57)
18	.46	(7.42)	.03	(0.50)
19	.35	(3.48)	.04	(0.18)

$R^2 = .73$ $F(41, 357) = 27.73$

$b_0 = 3.75$

$b_3 = -0.04 \ (-1.13)$

$b_4 = 0.05 \ (1.26)$

$b_5 = 0.001 \ (0.71)$

t-statistics are in parentheses

Equation 2-1

Compensation Definition: REMUN
Profitability Definition: Rate of Return on Equity

Firm (i)	b_1		b_2	
1	0.44	(7.25)	-0.005	(-0.89)
2	.47	(12.13)	.01	(0.13)
3	.51	(5.32)	.25	(0.83)
4	.46	(9.93)	-.09	(-0.62)
5	.29	(7.33)	-.80	(-6.64)
6	.36	(6.60)	-.34	(-2.79)
7	.58	(10.25)	.50	(2.45)
8	.57	(12.35)	.25	(4.19)
9	.65	(11.33)	.37	(2.98)
10	.90	(7.95)	1.64	(3.99)
11	.54	(9.43)	.02	(0.09)
12	.50	(7.61)	-.11	(-0.73)
13	.32	(8.80)	-.81	(-6.04)
14	.59	(11.20)	.32	(2.99)
15	.54	(7.36)	.09	(0.55)
16	.78	(6.98)	.74	(2.33)
17	.53	(9.74)	.09	(0.59)
18	.42	(8.79)	-.27	(-2.20)
19	.39	(6.90)	.01	(0.10)

R^2 = .83   F(41, 357) = 47.20

b_0 = 3.58

b_3 = -0.12 (-5.34)

b_4 = 0.002 (0.11)

b_5 = 0.002 (1.61)

t-statistics are in parentheses

Equation 2-1

Compensation Definition: TREM
Profitability Definition: Rate of Return on Equity

Firm (i)	b_1		b_2	
1	0.42	(6.65)	−0.02	(−0.22)
2	.49	(12.12)	.09	(0.93)
3	.55	(5.45)	.37	(1.16)
4	.28	(5.63)	−0.75	(−4.89)
5	.32	(7.81)	−.70	(−5.56)
6	.42	(7.23)	−.23	(−1.80)
7	.63	(10.55)	.52	(2.42)
8	.57	(11.69)	.26	(4.15)
9	.64	(10.62)	.36	(2.75)
10	.91	(7.62)	1.66	(3.85)
11	.58	(9.69)	.14	(0.72)
12	.50	(7.25)	−.08	(−0.52)
13	.32	(8.39)	−.79	(−5.63)
14	.59	(10.58)	.33	(2.87)
15	.55	(7.07)	.11	(0.67)
16	.78	(6.67)	.76	(2.27)
17	.51	(8.91)	−.001	(−0.01)
18	.43	(8.60)	−.23	(−1.73)
19	.42	(7.06)	.08	(0.66)

$R^2 = .83$ $F(41, 357) = 47.31$

$b_0 = 3.60$

$b_3 = -0.10 \ (-4.56)$

$b_4 = 0.03 \ (1.35)$

$b_5 = 0.001 \ (0.81)$

t-statistics are in parentheses

Equation 2-1

Compensation Definition: COMPN
Profitability Definition: Rate of Return on Equity

Firm (i)	b_1		b_2	
1	0.57	(5.90)	-0.12	(-0.85)
2	.62	(9.95)	-.10	(-0.68)
3	.56	(3.64)	-.12	(-0.25)
4	.34	(4.55)	-1.30	(-5.53)
5	.51	(8.14)	-.98	(-5.11)
6	.53	(6.04)	-.38	(-1.95)
7	.72	(7.93)	.24	(0.74)
8	.73	(9.80)	.14	(1.49)
9	.77	(8.35)	.23	(1.15)
10	.94	(5.20)	1.27	(1.94)
11	.68	(7.46)	-.09	(-0.31)
12	.65	(6.27)	-.16	(-0.67)
13	.70	(12.22)	-.53	(-2.49)
14	.71	(8.39)	.15	(0.86)
15	.67	(5.74)	-.05	(-0.20)
16	1.11	(6.22)	1.14	(2.24)
17	.57	(6.61)	-.40	(-1.69)
18	.49	(6.44)	-.61	(-3.08)
19	.57	(6.34)	.12	(-0.70)

$R^2 = .73$ $F(41, 357) = 27.43$

$b_0 = 3.14$

$b_3 = -0.08 \ (-2.27)$

$b_4 = -0.002 \ (-0.07)$

$b_5 = -0.001 \ (-0.50)$

t-statistics are in parentheses

Equation 2-1

Compensation Definition: CMPN
Profitability Definition: Rate of Return on Equity

Firm (i)	b_1		b_2	
1	0.66	(6.22)	-0.16	(-1.02)
2	.68	(10.01)	-.21	(-1.25)
3	.59	(3.56)	-.27	(-0.50)
4	.38	(4.67)	-1.46	(-5.73)
5	.56	(8.22)	-1.14	(-5.46)
6	.60	(6.23)	-.46	(-2.17)
7	.76	(7.75)	.10	(0.28)
8	.82	(10.06)	.12	(1.15)
9	1.06	(10.50)	.61	(2.83)
10	.97	(4.91)	1.09	(1.52)
11	.74	(7.41)	-.21	(-0.68)
12	.72	(6.33)	-.22	(-0.87)
13	.81	(13.00)	-.58	(-2.51)
14	.77	(8.29)	.04	(0.19)
15	.74	(5.77)	-.13	(-0.48)
16	1.87	(9.63)	2.99	(5.39)
17	.72	(7.64)	-.23	(-0.92)
18	.58	(7.03)	-.63	(-2.89)
19	.64	(6.55)	.11	(0.60)

$R^2 = .73$ $F(41, 357) = 27.53$

$b_0 = 2.89$

$b_3 = -0.08 \ (-2.17)$

$b_4 = -0.001 \ (-0.20)$

$b_5 = -0.001 \ (-0.41)$

t-statistics are in parentheses

Equation 2-2

Compensation Definition: REMUN
Profitability Definition: Rate of Return on Assets

Firm (i)	c_1	c_2	c_3
1	0.30 (5.54)	−0.12 (−1.19)	−0.02 (−0.50)
2	.42 (9.72)	.09 (0.72)	−0.01 (−0.40)
3	.42 (4.79)	.25 (1.00)	.02 (0.63)
4	.43 (5.45)	.14 (0.58)	.02 (0.63)
5	.26 (6.68)	−.72 (−5.94)	−.02 (−0.67)
6	.29 (5.43)	−.27 (−1.85)	−.01 (−0.28)
7	.44 (8.58)	.29 (2.43)	.02 (0.46)
8	.49 (9.76)	.39 (4.61)	.07 (2.18)
9	.67 (11.15)	.68 (5.75)	.04 (1.12)
10	.55 (5.54)	.74 (2.47)	.09 (1.19)
11	.45 (5.25)	.08 (0.30)	.02 (0.49)
12	.42 (7.37)	−.10 (−0.84)	−.01 (−0.31)
13	.24 (6.18)	−.69 (−5.54)	.03 (0.98)
14	.67 (10.79)	.92 (8.09)	.11 (3.11)
15	.43 (4.65)	.14 (1.04)	.07 (1.55)
16	.69 (8.32)	.61 (3.60)	−.06 (−1.46)
17	.60 (9.92)	.79 (5.47)	.09 (2.33)
18	.38 (8.73)	−.00 (−0.01)	.04 (1.29)
19	.32 (5.32)	.03 (0.22)	.01 (0.18)

$R^2 = .86$ $\qquad$ $F(60, 338) = 40.58$

$c_0 = 3.77$

$c_4 = -0.08 \ (-3.95)$

$c_5 = 0.03 \ (1.65)$

$c_6 = 0.004 \ (3.84)$

t-statistics are in parentheses

Equation 2-2

Compensation Definition: TREM
Profitability Definition: Rate of Return on Assets

Firm (i)	c_1		c_2		c_3	
1	0.25	(4.38)	−0.14	(−1.36)	−0.02	(−0.36)
2	.43	(9.66)	.26	(2.09)	−0.01	(−0.14)
3	.38	(4.13)	.21	(0.81)	.04	(0.86)
4	.24	(2.97)	−.60	(−2.43)	−.02	(−0.57)
5	.27	(6.74)	−.51	(−4.08)	−.004	(−0.13)
6	.32	(5.40)	−.07	(−0.47)	.03	(0.69)
7	.43	(8.19)	.39	(3.10)	.08	(2.20)
8	.45	(8.73)	.42	(4.72)	.08	(2.45)
9	.67	(10.70)	.76	(6.23)	.04	(1.14)
10	.53	(5.23)	.80	(2.59)	.10	(1.22)
11	.48	(5.42)	.29	(1.00)	.01	(0.27)
12	.39	(6.72)	−.06	(−0.46)	−.01	(−0.14)
13	.25	(6.20)	−.56	(−4.35)	.01	(0.46)
14	.67	(10.48)	1.01	(8.61)	.10	(2.92)
15	.43	(4.50)	.22	(1.58)	.06	(1.31)
16	.69	(8.07)	.71	(4.06)	−.06	(−1.56)
17	.61	(9.82)	.95	(6.42)	.11	(2.77)
18	.35	(7.65)	.01	(0.16)	.04	(1.26)
19	.28	(4.62)	.03	(0.21)	.03	(0.69)

$R^2 = .86$ $F(60, 338) = 42.27$

$c_0 = 3.89$

$c_4 = -0.06 \ (-3.10)$

$c_5 = 0.05 \ (2.32)$

$c_6 = 0.003 \ (3.08)$

t-statistics are in parentheses

Equation 2-2

Compensation Definition: COMPN
Profitability Definition: Rate of Return on Assets

Firm (i)	c_1		c_2		c_3	
1	0.16	(1.77)	−0.18	(−1.09)	−0.01	(−0.14)
2	.41	(5.69)	.36	(1.76)	−0.004	(−0.06)
3	.30	(2.02)	.11	(0.26)	.05	(0.69)
4	.34	(2.59)	−.11	(−0.26)	.03	(0.45)
5	.26	(4.04)	−.22	(−1.06)	.12	(2.30)
6	.27	(2.79)	.001	(0.01)	.04	(0.66)
7	.39	(4.57)	.42	(2.05)	.09	(1.44)
8	.38	(4.47)	.34	(2.36)	.10	(1.79)
9	.68	(6.68)	.93	(4.64)	.03	(0.62)
10	.50	(3.01)	.85	(1.68)	.10	(0.75)
11	.42	(2.91)	.31	(0.66)	.01	(0.19)
12	.38	(3.95)	.02	(0.10)	.01	(0.12)
13	.72	(11.02)	.40	(1.91)	−.14	(−3.21)
14	.70	(6.68)	1.22	(6.34)	.11	(1.87)
15	.36	(2.30)	.22	(0.94)	.10	(1.25)
16	.88	(6.32)	1.29	(4.50)	.11	(1.66)
17	.58	(5.70)	1.07	(4.44)	.16	(2.55)
18	.31	(4.19)	.02	(0.36)	.04	(0.70)
19	.25	(2.41)	.05	(0.21)	.03	(0.45)

R^2 = .75 $F_{(60, 338)}$ = 21.10

c_0 = 4.03

c_4 = −0.02 (−0.73)

c_5 = 0.04 (1.06)

c_6 = 0.002 (1.16)

t-statistics are in parentheses

Equation 2-2

Compensation Definition: CMPN
Profitability Definition: Rate of Return on Assets

Firm (i)	c_1		c_2		c_3	
1	0.21	(2.21)	-0.16	(-0.89)	-0.01	(-0.14)
2	.43	(5.37)	.29	(1.31)	-.004	(-0.06)
3	.34	(2.08)	.13	(0.27)	.04	(0.60)
4	.38	(2.63)	-.13	(-0.29)	.02	(0.30)
5	.28	(3.85)	-.35	(-1.57)	.12	(2.03)
6	.31	(2.84)	-.05	(-0.17)	.04	(0.46)
7	.42	(4.46)	.39	(1.76)	.08	(1.24)
8	.41	(4.41)	.32	(2.05)	.10	(1.62)
9	.96	(8.62)	1.37	(6.20)	.01	(0.10)
10	.53	(2.87)	.81	(1.47)	.10	(0.67)
11	.46	(2.89)	.29	(0.57)	.01	(0.16)
12	.39	(3.76)	-.02	(-0.11)	.002	(0.03)
13	.82	(11.44)	.40	(1.74)	-.17	(-3.59)
14	.69	(6.05)	1.12	(5.31)	.11	(1.76)
15	.35	(2.07)	.13	(0.53)	.10	(1.26)
16	1.46	(9.53)	2.43	(7.77)	-.24	(-3.28)
17	.69	(6.17)	1.24	(4.65)	.14	(2.04)
18	.36	(4.46)	.03	(0.46)	.03	(0.55)
19	.27	(2.39)	.02	(0.08)	.04	(0.46)

R^2 = .75 $F(60, 338)$ = 20.84

c_0 =   3.92

c_4 =

c_5 =   0.04 (1.21)

c_6 =   0.003 (1.46)

t-statistics are in parentheses

Equation 2-2

Compensation Definition: REMUN
Profitability Definition: Rate of Return on Equity

Firm (i)	c_1		c_2		c_3	
1	0.47	(7.45)	0.01	(0.09)	0.02	(0.27)
2	.50	(9.90)	-.07	(-0.67)	-.03	(-0.93)
3	.52	(4.91)	.23	(0.77)	.01	(0.35)
4	.45	(7.15)	-.17	(-1.11)	.03	(0.65)
5	.30	(6.48)	-.86	(-6.80)	.005	(0.16)
6	.39	(6.69)	-.40	(-2.94)	-.03	(-0.65)
7	.58	(8.50)	.44	(2.16)	.02	(0.39)
8	.54	(9.09)	.24	(4.03)	.08	(2.19)
9	.65	(10.28)	.38	(2.98)	.03	(1.04)
10	.94	(5.97)	1.68	(3.39)	-.02	(-0.20)
11	.55	(8.27)	-.01	(-0.03)	.02	(0.48)
12	.50	(7.53)	-.21	(-1.30)	-0.03	(-0.66)
13	.26	(6.52)	-.86	(-6.23)	.07	(2.29)
14	.55	(9.62)	.43	(3.68)	.14	(3.73)
15	.45	(4.72)	-.05	(-0.33)	.08	(1.90)
16	.79	(6.38)	.68	(2.12)	-.01	(-0.30)
17	.46	(7.51)	.08	(0.52)	.14	(3.50)
18	.41	(7.17)	-.29	(-2.31)	.04	(1.34)
19	.41	(6.21)	-.002	(-0.02)	.002	(0.05)

$R^2 = .84$ $F(60, 338) = 35.48$

$c_0 = 3.49$

$c_4 = -0.109 \ (-5.09)$

$c_5 = 0.01 \ (0.41)$

$c_6 = 0.003 \ (2.98)$

t-statistics are in parentheses

Equation 2-2

Compensation Definition: TREM
Profitability Definition: Rate of Return on Equity

Firm (i)	c_1		c_2		c_3	
1	0.45	(6.85)	0.000	(0.01)	0.02	(0.29)
2	.52	(9.86)	.02	(0.20)	-.03	(-0.84)
3	.57	(5.16)	.40	(1.26)	.01	(0.32)
4	.29	(4.44)	-.79	(-5.05)	.004	(-0.10)
5	.32	(6.74)	-.74	(-5.68)	.01	(0.46)
6	.43	(7.11)	-.24	(-1.72)	.004	(0.08)
7	.55	(7.77)	.37	(1.82)	.08	(2.15)
8	.52	(8.45)	1.71	(4.04)	.09	(2.41)
9	.64	(9.67)	.13	(2.86)	.04	(1.08)
10	.94	(5.74)	1.71	(3.32)	.01	(-0.16)
11	.59	(8.58)	.13	(0.68)	.01	(0.38)
12	.49	(7.14)	-.17	(-1.04)	-.02	(-0.49)
13	.26	(6.16)	-.83	(-5.78)	.07	(2.28)
14	.54	(9.16)	.44	(3.59)	.14	(3.46)
15	.45	(4.50)	-.03	(-0.20)	.08	(1.81)
16	.79	(6.09)	.69	(2.08)	-.01	(-0.21)
17	.41	(6.50)	.000	(0.00)	.17	(4.20)
18	.41	(6.95)	-.24	(-1.87)	.05	(1.32)
19	.42	(6.18)	.06	(0.49)	.02	(0.39)

$R^2 = .84$ $F(60, 338) = 36.37$

$c_0 = 3.53$

$c_4 = -0.11 \; (-4.72)$

$c_5 = 0.03 \; (1.30)$

$c_6 = 0.002 \; (2.31)$

t-statistics are in parentheses

Equation 2-2

Compensation Definition: COMPN
Profitability Definition: Rate of Return on Equity

Firm (i)	c_1		c_2		c_3	
1	0.53	(5.22)	−0.05	(−0.23)	0.03	(0.37)
2	.61	(7.48)	−.10	(−0.62)	−.06	(−0.91)
3	.54	(3.11)	−.01	(−0.02)	.02	(0.32)
4	.23	(2.26)	−1.29	(−5.26)	.09	(1.30)
5	.40	(5.42)	−.81	(−3.98)	.12	(2.33)
6	.50	(5.26)	−.35	(−1.58)	−.01	(−0.15)
7	.60	(5.44)	.22	(0.64)	.09	(1.44)
8	.61	(6.29)	.14	(1.50)	.09	(1.69)
9	.73	(7.11)	.33	(1.62)	.03	(0.54)
10	1.00	(3.90)	1.57	(1.95)	−.04	(−0.32)
11	.65	(6.02)	−.01	(−0.02)	.01	(0.26)
12	.60	(5.56)	−.20	(−0.77)	−.02	(−0.30)
13	.71	(10.96)	−.45	(−2.02)	−.04	(−0.92)
14	.62	(6.77)	.33	(1.75)	.13	(2.06)
15	.49	(3.15)	−.17	(−0.66)	.10	(1.53)
16	1.09	(5.38)	1.20	(1.93)	−.01	(−0.19)
17	.40	(4.01)	−.30	(−1.26)	.23	(3.65)
18	.42	(4.64)	−.54	(−2.72)	.04	(0.82)
19	.52	(4.91)	.11	(0.60)	.01	(0.18)

R^2 = .74 $F(60, 338) = 20.16$

c_0 = 3.26

c_4 = −0.08 (−2.25)

c_5 = 0.002 (0.06)

c_6 = 0.001 (0.48)

t-statistics are in parentheses

Equation 2-2

Compensation Definition:	CMPN	
Profitability Definition:	Rate of Return on Equity	

Firm (i)	c_1	c_2	c_3
1	0.62 (5.50)	−0.09 (−0.42)	0.03 (0.30)
2	.68 (7.57)	−.21 (−1.17)	−.07 (−1.00)
3	.58 (3.05)	−.15 (−0.27)	.02 (0.25)
4	.27 (2.44)	−1.45 (−5.37)	.09 (1.17)
5	.46 (5.61)	−.96 (−4.30)	.12 (2.08)
6	.57 (5.45)	−.45 (−1.87)	−.03 (−0.38)
7	.65 (5.34)	.07 (0.20)	.09 (1.29)
8	.70 (6.58)	.12 (1.16)	.09 (1.47)
9	1.04 (9.19)	.71 (3.18)	.002 (0.04)
10	1.05 (3.72)	1.44 (1.63)	−.06 (−0.40)
11	.70 (5.95)	−.13 (−0.42)	.01 (0.23)
12	.67 (5.65)	−.27 (−0.96)	−.03 (−0.40)
13	.85 (11.90)	−.50 (−2.06)	−.07 (−1.33)
14	.69 (6.78)	.21 (1.02)	.12 (1.70)
15	.56 (3.30)	−.24 (−0.82)	.10 (1.34)
16	1.93 (8.71)	3.18 (5.58)	−.06 (−0.94)
17	.56 (5.16)	−.13 (−0.48)	.22 (3.07)
18	.52 (5.17)	−.56 (−2.52)	.04 (0.67)
19	.59 (5.11)	.11 (0.55)	.01 (0.15)

$R^2 = .74$ $F(60, 338) = 19.79$

$c_0 = 3.01$

$c_4 = -0.08 \ (-2.08)$

$c_5 = -0.01 \ (-0.14)$

$c_6 = 0.001 \ (0.37)$

t-statistics are in parentheses

Appendix C

Executive Compensation Sample

The following nineteen firms make up the sample used in the statistical analysis of executive compensation.

Archer-Daniels-Midland

Beatrice Foods

Borden

CPC International

Coca-Cola

Del Monte

General Foods

General Mills

Heinz

Kraftco

Nabisco

National Distillers & Chemical

Pepsico

Pet

Pillsbury

Quaker Oats

Ralston-Purina

Standard Brands

Swift (Esmark)

Appendix D

Profitability Sample

The following firms make up the sample used in the statistical analysis of profitability.

American Broadcasting Company

Archer-Daniel-Midland

Armco Steel

Babcock & Wilcox

Borden

Burlington Industries

Burroughs

Celanese

Dana

Dart

Ford Motor

Getty Oil

Heinz

Honeywell

Hormel

Ingersoll-Rand

IBM

Kaiser Aluminum & Chemical

Kimberly-Clark

Mobil Oil

Northrop

Pepsico

Pet

Ralston-Purina

Texas Instruments

Uniroyal

White Motor

Appendix E

Profitability Variable Definitions and Sources of Data

Rate of Return on Equity represents profits (net income) divided by the value of common equity.

Net Income represents income after all operating and non-operating income and expense and minority interest but before preferred and common dividends as reported by Compustat.

Common Equity represents the value of common stock as reported by Compustat.

Industry Rate of Return represents profits divided by total book value as reported in *Standard & Poor's Industry Studies.* This was weighted by each firm's sales to calculate that firm's industry rate of return.

Market Portfolio Rate of Return represents profits divided by equity for all firms as reported in the *Economic Report of the President.*

Risk Free Interest Rate represents the average yield on three month treasury bills as reported in the *Economic Report of the President.*

Sales represents gross sales and other operating revenue less discounts, returns, and allowances as reported by Compustat.

Debt represents debt obligations due after one year as reported by Compustat.

Diversification represents the number of four digit SIC industries in which the firm operated as reported by *Dun & Bradstreet's.*

Appendix F

Difference in Regression Residuals

Difference Between the Regression Residual in the Year an M-form Organization was Adopted and the Regression Residual Five Years Later

(100 = 1% change in return on equity)

Firm	IRR	IRRS	IRRSDE	IRRSDED*	CAPM	CAPMS	CAPMSD
ABC	179	364	− 23	− 827	− 222	− 217	− 476
Archer-Danials-Midland	− 438	− 470	− 326	− 326	− 34	− 29	142
Armco Steel	66	16	− 72	− 72	150	376	230
Babcock & Wilcox	− 364	− 161	87	6	− 280	− 139	− 53
Borden	4	0	19	19	115	172	90
Burlington	117	− 67	− 60	− 60	− 204	− 262	− 218
Burroughs	374	2	28	28	341	436	66
Celanese	− 118	− 155	183	− 170	− 496	− 332	− 184
Dana	− 336	− 152	− 158	− 158	− 58	− 30	− 172
Dart	1487	1851	713	174	2245	1686	378
Ford Motor	390	215	319	319	− 232	−1534	− 206
Getty Oil	− 469	− 470	− 490	− 468	− 359	− 344	− 395
Heinz	101	− 106	− 113	− 125	174	152	95
Honeywell	114	220	241	260	− 456	− 92	91
Hormel	54	151	− 55	− 150	386	391	− 138
Ingersoll-Rand	63	229	245	138	448	471	− 14
IBM	227	245	134	134	410	450	309
Kaiser Aluminum	104	147	212	212	132	137	60
Kimberly-Clark	− 29	25	46	32	143	− 83	79
Mobil Oil	92	− 3	7	19	156	116	144
Northrop	− 668	− 649	− 529	− 529	−1037	− 898	− 416
Pepsico	− 261	− 97	− 40	50	− 257	− 132	16
Pet	− 178	− 197	− 186	− 14	62	58	65
Ralston-Purina	320	249	260	260	323	322	258
Texas Instruments	− 558	− 332	− 97		− 793	− 640	
Uniroyal	− 157	111	− 114	49	− 671	− 484	− 164
White Motor	−1467	−1325	− 579	− 354	− 860	− 900	− 126

---

* Texas Instruments was dropped from the sample when a diversification variable was added because of insufficient data.

where:

      IRR = regression where dependent variable is the difference between the firm's rate of return and that of a weighted average of its industries

    IRRS = IRR + sales

  IRRSDE = IRRS + debt-equity ratio

IRRSDED = IRRSDE + diversification

    CAPM = capital asset pricing model

  CAPMS = CAPM + sales

 CAPMSD = CAPMS + diversification

Appendix G: Coefficients of Dummy Variables

Estimated Coefficients of Dummy Variables Representing the Use of an M-form Organization

(100 = 1% change in return on equity)

Firm	IRR	IRRS	IRRSDE	IRRSDED*	CAPM	CAPMS	CAPMSD*
ABC	-513.1 (-1.79)	-952.8 (-1.56)	-1534.9 (-2.80)	-465.3 (-0.64)	-57.5 (-0.42)	-401.8 (-1.64)	-181.6 (-0.64)
Archer-Danials-Midland	-199.0 (-0.49)	-480.6 (-3.07)	-408.3 (-2.59)	22.5 (0.001)	-156.8 (-0.61)	-242.0 (-1.10)	0.01 (0.001)
Armco Steel	6.2 (0.10)	-145.1 (-1.29)	-45.8 (-0.25)	186.2 (1.68)	-294.5 (-3.23)	-196.6 (-1.23)	-245.2 (-1.10)
Babcock & Wilcox	-110.4 (-0.82)	263.3 (1.99)	166.1 (1.01)	179.4 (0.91)	-231.5 (-2.30)	-178.4 (-1.08)	38.0 (0.16)
Borden	-25.0 (-0.62)	-146.2 (-2.02)	-232.6 (-2.93)	-135.2 (-0.94)	-168.6 (-2.16)	-291.2 (-1.93)	-72.6 (-0.57)
Burlington	95.6 (1.67)	127.9 (1.32)	128.4 (1.30)	-474.7 (-3.07)	91.0 (0.80)	265.6 (1.17)	-370.3 (-2.50)
Burroughs	501.1 (4.95)	470.1 (2.87)	502.2 (2.84)	173.2 (0.43)	356.9 (4.74)	426.3 (3.25)	46.2 (0.10)
Celanese	0.05 (0.001)	-79.9 (-0.62)	-77.1 (-0.57)	224.3 (2.41)	-198.5 (-1.98)	41.7 (0.31)	516.3 (3.52)
Mobil Oil	243.9 (2.80)	93.8 (3.37)	89.1 (3.39)	-101.8 (-0.63)	-4.61 (-0.06)	-104.9 (-1.55)	15.0 (0.06)

Firm	IRR	IRRS	IRRSDE	IRRSDED*	CAPM	CAPMS	CAPMSD*
Northrop	-446.4 (-2.69)	422.5 (-2.30)	-386.3 (-2.56)	-92.1 (-0.89)	-718.5 (-3.29)	-458.2 (-3.49)	-116.7 (-1.24)
Pepsico	-602.1 (-5.31)	-309.1 (-1.94)	-129.4 (-0.73)	-468.7 (-1.19)	-496.0 (-4.49)	-454.0 (-2.10)	-272.5 (-0.93)
Pet	-57.6 (-0.78)	-146.9 (-1.57)	-82.9 (-0.81)	-316.7 (-0.91)	53.6 (0.71)	-105.7 (-1.21)	-30.3 (-0.78)
Ralston-Purina	99.6 (1.01)	-11.1 (-0.05)	-205.6 (-1.00)	-1360.4 (0.000)	-20.4 (-0.20)	-304.8 (-1.75)	3096.0 (0.000)
Texas Instruments	-558.1 (-1.54)	-332.7 (-2.11)	-97.5 (-2.01)		-793.0 (-1.66)	-640.1 (-1.77)	
Uniroyal	-94.3 (-1.16)	-43.5 (-0.46)	-43.4 (-0.44)	-299.1 (-2.48)	-307.6 (-2.70)	-260.9 (-1.93)	-320.3 (-0.62)
White Motor	-333.3 (-1.55)	34.6 (0.07)	-176.9 (-0.52)	-45.6 (-0.09)	-288.3 (-1.61)	-328.8 (-0.80)	-258.9 (-0.59)

(numbers in parentheses are t-statistics)

---

* Texas Instruments was dropped from the sample when a diversification variable was added because of insufficient data.

where:

IRR = regression where dependent variable is the
difference between the firm's rate of
return and that of a weighted average of
its industries

IRRS = IRR + sales

IRRSDE = IRRS + debt-equity ratio

IRRSDED = IRRSDE + diversification

CAPM = capital asset pricing model

CAPMS = CAPM + sales

CAPMSD = CAPMS + diversification

Appendix H

Classifications of Sample Corporations

Alcoa	1935-68	U
	1968-73	M
American Brands	1935-63	U-H
	1963-66	$\overline{\text{M}}$-H
	1966-73	X
American Broadcast	1942-53	U
	1953-66	U-H
	1966-73	M
American Can	1935-56	U
	1956-64	H
	1964-68	U
	1969-73	M
AMF	1935-58	U-H
	1958-73	M
Anaconda	1935-71	H
	1971-73	M
Anheuser-Busch	1950-72	U-H
Archer-Daniels-Midland	1950-56	U (or U-H)
	1957-72	M
Armco Steel	1935-67	U-H
	1967-73	M
Ashland Oil	1936-51	U
	1951-66	U-H
	1967-73	M'
Avon Products	1935-70	U
	1971-73	U-H
Babcock & Wilcox	1935-58	U-H
	1958-63	M'
	1963-73	M
Beatrice Foods	1935-73	M

Bendix	1935-64	H
	1965-68	M
	1969	H
	1970-73	M
Bethlehem Steel	1935-73	U-H
Boeing	1935-60	$\underline{U}$
	1960-71	$\overline{M}$
	1971-73	M
Borden	1935-67	M'
	1967-73	M
Borg-Warner	1935-70	H
	1970-73	M
Brown Group	1935-51	U
	1952-70	U-H
	1971-73	M
Brunswick	1935-59	U
	1959-73	M
Burlington Industries	1935-53	U-H (or H)
	1954-62	M'
	1962-73	M
Burroughs	1935-57	U (or U-H)
	1957-60	M'
	1960-65	U
	1965-73	M
Campbell Soup	1950-68	$\underline{U}$ (or U-H)
	1969-72	$\overline{M}$
Carrier	1935-53	U
	1953-73	M
Castle & Cooke	1935-57	?
	1958-72	H
	1972-74	X
Caterpillar Tractor	1935-73	U
Celanese	1935-41	U
	1942-46	U-H
	1947-59	$\overline{M}$
	1960-61	M'
	1962-73	M
Chrysler	1935-55	U
	1955-57	$\overline{M}$
	1958-73	U (or U-H)
Coca-Cola	1935-67	U-H
	1968-73	M

Corning Glass	1935-39	U
	1939-49	M'
	1949-73	M
CPC International	1950-58	U (2 companies-both U)
	1958-66	U
	1967-73	M
Cummins Engine	1935-58	U
	1958-67	U-H
	1968-69	M'
	1970-73	U-H
Dana	Until 1964	U
	1964-74	M
Dart Industries	Until 1949	U
	1949-61	U-H
	1962-73	M
Deere	1935-54	U
	1954-69	U-H
	1970-73	M'
Del Monte	1935-65	U
	1966-72	U-H
	1972-73	M'
Dow Chemical	1935-63	U-H
	1963-73	$\overline{M}$
DuPont	1935-73	M
Esmark	Until 1968	U-H
	1968-69	M'
	1970-73	M
Firestone Tire	1935-73	X
Ford Motor	Until 1946	U
	1946-62	M'
	1963-73	M
Freuhauf	Until 1961	U-H
	1961-67	M'
	1968-73	M
General Electric	1935-46	U
	1946-51	M'
	1951-73	M
General Foods	1935	H
	1936-46	U (or U-H)
	1946-52	M'
	1952-73	M
General Mills	1935-37	H
	1937-73	M

Getty Oil	1935-49	H
	1949-59	M̄
	1959-73	M
Gulf Oil	1935-55	U
	1956-68	M'
	1968-73	M
Heinz	Until 1966	U-H (or H)
	1966-74	M
Hercules	1935-73	M
Honeywell	1935-41	U
	1941-61	M̄
	1961-73	M
Hormel (George)	1935-65	M'
	1965-73	M
Ingersoll-Rand	1935-64	U
	1964-73	M
Inland Steel	1935-73	U-H (or X)
IBM	1936-56	U
	1956-66	M'
	1966-72	M
Johns-Manville	1935-46	U
	1946-73	M
Johnson & Johnson	1935-73	M
Kaiser Aluminum & Chemical	Until 1957	U (or U-H)
	1957-73	M
Kellogg	Until 1968	U
	1969-74	U-H
Kennecott Copper	1936-67	U-H
	1968-73	X (with one division H)
Kimberly-Clark	1935-49	U
	1950-60	U-H
	1960-65	M̄
	1965-73	M
Kraftco	1935-73	H
Liggett & Myers	Until 1964	U
	1964-69	X
	1970-73	M
Lilly (Eli)	1935-73	U-H
Marathon Oil	1935-73	U-H
Minnesota Mining (3M)	1935-44	U
	1944-48	U (or X)
	1948-73	M

Mobil Oil	Until 1959	U-H
	1959-73	M
Monsanto	1935-38	$\underline{U}$
	1939-68	$\overline{M}$
	1968-71	M'
	1971-73	M
Motorola	Until 1941	U
	1946-56	$\overline{M}$
	1956-68	M'
	1968-73	M
Nabisco	Until 1962	U (or U-H)
	1963-73	U-H (or X)
NL Industries	Until 1968	U-H
	1968-73	M
National Distillers	Until 1950	U (or U-H)
and Chemical	1951-73	M
Northrop	1939-1959	H
	1959-73	M
Ogden	1935-62	H
	1963-69	M'
	1969-73	M
Otis Elevator	1935-73	U-H
Pepsico	1950-64	U (or U-H)
	1964-73	M
Pet	1935-59	U (or U-H)
	1959-61	M'
	1961-73	M
Pillsbury	Until 1958	U
	1958-68	M'
	1969-73	M
Proctor & Gamble	Until 1956	$\underline{U}$ (or U-H)
	1956-66	$\overline{M}$ (or M')
	1966-73	M
Pullman	Until 1964	H
	1964-73	M'
Quaker Oats	1935-41	U
	1942-70	U-H (may be X since 1966)
	1970-73	M
Ralston-Purina	Until 1956	U
	1956-64	U-H
	1965-66	M'
	1967-72	M
Reynolds Metals	Until 1969	$\underline{U}$
	1969-74	$\overline{M}$

Standards Brands	1935-56	U
	1956-69	U-H
	1969-74	M′
	1974	M
St. Regis Paper	1935-63	U (or U-H)
	1964-69	M′
	1969-74	M
Sun Oil	Until 1969	U
	1970-71	M′
	1971-74	M
Texas Instruments	1935-51	U
	1951-53	U-H
	1954-56	M′
	1957-73	M
Uniroyal	1935-57	$\overline{M}$
	1957-60	M′
	1960-73	M
U.S. Gypsum	Until 1965	U-H
	1960-67	M′ (or M)
	1968-73	M (or M′)
U.S. Industries	Until 1950	U
	1950-73	H (may be M′ since 1969)
White Motor	1935-53	U
	1954-64	U-H
	1965-73	M
Zenith Radio	1935-73	U (or U-H)

Notes

Chapter 1

1. Alfred D. Chandler, Jr., *Strategy and Structure: Chapters in the History of the American Industrial Enterprise,* (Cambridge, Massachusetts: The MIT Press, 1962).

2. Williamson has written often about the multidivisional organization. See: *Markets and Hierarchies: Analysis and Antitrust Considerations,* (New York: The Free Press, 1975).

3. Ibid., p. 150.

4. Based on "Assessing and Classifying the Internal Structure and Control Apparatus of the Modern Corporation," Oliver E. Williamson and Narotum Bhargava, in *Market Structure and Corporate Behavior: Theory and Empirical Analysis of the Firm,* Keith Cowling, ed., (London: Gray-Mills Publishing Ltd., 1972), pp. 125-48.

5. Chandler, *Strategy and Structure,* p. 16.

6. Ibid., p. 291.

7. Ibid., p. 286.

8. Ibid., pp. 295-96.

9. Ibid., pp. 296-97.

10. Ibid., p. 299.

11. For example, the sales department might perceive itself as being a sales maximizer, while the manufacturing department might perceive itself as being a cost minimizer.

12. Including forming new divisions in new markets.

13. Of course, if a division performed poorly over an extended period the general office needed the capacity to correct the slide. If the division operated in a declining market, it might be phased out. If the division's reduced profitability was correctible, the general office, through its staff, might take over the running of the division for a limited time. It needs to be stressed that such involvement by the general office in the day-to-day affairs of a division was unusual.

14. Oliver E. Williamson, "Managerial Discretion, Organization Form, and the Multi-Division Hypothesis," in *The Corporate Economy,* Robin Marris and Adrian Wood, ed., 1971, pp. 343-86.

15. Williamson, *Markets and Hierarchies,* pp. 345-46.

16. Anthony Downs, *Inside Bureaucracy,* (Boston: Little, Brown and Company, 1966), p. 118.

17. Herbert Simon, *Administrative Behavior,* Second Edition, (New York: The Free Press, 1957), p. 155.

18. Chester Bernard, *The Functions of the Executive,* (Cambridge, Massachusetts: Harvard University Press, 1938), p. 106.

19. Williamson, *Markets and Hierarchies,* p. 346.

20. Williamson, "Managerial Discretion, Organization Form, and the Multi-Division Hypothesis," p. 347.

21. There are some exceptions to this rule. The most important exception occurs when one of the divisions is a monopoly supplier of an input to other divisions in the firm. If the supply division were a profit center it would transfer its product at a price greater than marginal cost to other divisions within the firm. It has been shown (see "On the Economics of Transfer Pricing," Jack Hirshleifer, *Journal of Business,* 1956) that the firm maximizes its profits when transfers within the firm occur at price equal to marginal cost. In a case of this type the supply division is given responsibility to minimize its cost for a particular output. That is, the supply division is established as a cost center.

22. Williamson, "Managerial Discretion, Organization Form, and the Multi-Division Hypothesis," p. 362.

Chapter 2

1. Adolf A. Berle and Gardiner C. Means, *The Modern Corporation and Private Property,* Revised Edition, (New York: Harcourt, Brace & World, Inc., 1968).

2. Yarrow, in *Market Structure and Corporate Behavior,* Keith Cowling, ed., 1972.

3. In a market with perfect mobility, the executive would be able to capture all of the additional profit.

4. Oliver E. Williamson, *The Economics of Discretionary Behavior: Managerial Objectives in a Theory of the Firm,* Englewood Cliffs, New Jersey: Prentice-Hall, 1964), p. 39.

5. William Baumol, *Behavior, Value and Growth,* (New York: The Macmillan Company, 1959).

6. Williamson, *The Economics of Discretionary Behavior,* Ch. 4.

7. Herbert A. Simon, "The Compensation of Executives," *Sociometry,* March, 1957. A more recent study of 150 financial executives concludes that the prime determinants of base salaries are the reporting level in the organization of the executive, the number of levels reporting to him, the executive's education and age, and the firm's sales and profits. The study was conducted by Graef S. Crystal. It was reported in the *Wall Street Journal* on February 27, 1978. The study is a confidential report for a client and is not available to the public.

8. See *Executive Compensation,* by David R. Roberts (Glencoe, Illinois: The Free Press, 1959). Roberts has made several observations that give some support to Simon. He has shown that executives seldom entertain offers of similar jobs. He says that this observation is consistent with low mobility and high variation of compensation, even among firms of the same size. Most promotion comes from within the firm. He further points out that the market for young executives is quite competitive, and that it is the starting rate not the top rate, of compensation which is important.

9. Williamson, *The Economics of Discretionary Behavior,* Ch. 4.

10.   Roberts, *Executive Compensation.*

11.   Joseph W. McGuire, John S. Y. Chiu, and Alvar O. Elbing, "Executive Incomes, Sales, and Profits," *American Economic Review,* September, 1962.

12.   Wilbur G. Lewellen and Blaine Huntsman, "Managerial Pay and Corporate Performance," *American Economic Review,* 1970.

13.   Yarrow, in *Market Structure and Corporate Behavior,* Keith Cowling, ed., 1972.

14.   Robert Masson, "Executive Motivations, Earnings, and Consequent Equity Performance," *Journal of Political Economy,* Nov./Dec., 1971.

15.   Wilbur G. Lewellen, *The Ownership Income of Management,* National Bureau of Economic Research—Fiscal Studies 14, (New York: National Bureau of Economic Research, 1971).

16.   Masson, "Executive Motivations, Earnings, and Consequent Equity Performance," p. 1284.

17.   The nineteen firms are listed in appendix C.

18.   Complete definitions are given in appendix A.

19.   It is pointed out by Chester Bernard (*The Functions of the Executive,* 1938) that inducements to executives can be of several types besides the traditional material form. Barnard adds: "Almost every type of incentive that can be, or is, necessary will itself in some degree call for material outgo. . . . Hence, the various incentives are in competition with each other even from the material point of view." If the board of directors (who must approve the compensation package) were to make up an optimal incentive package, the tradeoff between these various types of incentives should be such that any increase in staff past the profit-maximizing level would cause a fall in compensation. This argument can be seen more easily if a utility function of the type used by Williamson (in *The Economies of Discretionary Behavior: Managerial Objectives in a Theory of the Firm*) is introduced.

$$\text{Let } U = U(s, m, \pi)$$

where:

$$s \;=\; \text{staff}$$

$$m \;=\; \text{managerial emoluments (salary)}$$

$$\pi \;=\; \text{firm profits}$$

If the compensation package is such that compensation is positively tied to profits and the executive is maximizing his utility then:

$$dU = \frac{\partial U}{\partial s}\, ds + \frac{\partial U}{\partial m}\, dm + \frac{\partial U}{\partial \pi}\, d\pi = 0$$

so

$$\frac{ds}{dm} = -\left[\left(\frac{\partial U}{\partial \pi} \Big/ \frac{\partial U}{\partial s} \right) \frac{d\pi}{dm} + \frac{\partial U}{\partial m} \Big/ \frac{\partial U}{\partial s} \right]$$

Since $\partial U/\partial m$, $\partial U/\partial s$, $\partial U/\partial \pi$ and $d\pi/dm$ are all positive, ds/dm is negative. The executive must choose between increased staff or increased firm profitability. Masson (in "Executive Motivations, Earnings, and Consequent Equity Performance"), makes the same argument.

20. It can be argued that, even in cross section, once the level of sales is accounted for executive compensation will increase with increased profitability. This line of reasoning has two problems: (1) profitability may depend to a large degree on the industry in which the firm operates, and (2) profitability is much more variable than sales. In any one year the level of profitability of a firm may bear little relation to its general level of profitability during the executive's tenure. It would be the general level of profitability which would be reflected in the level of compensation.

21. Masson, "Executive Motivations, Earnings, and Consequent Equity Performance."

22. Since the elasticity estimates are being used to form a sample population in which certain hypotheses are tested, the significance of the individual estimates need not be a matter of concern. The test involves the distribution of the population of elasticities. When the zero test is performed on only those estimates that are significant, the results remain essentially the same.

23. J. Fred Weston and Surenda Mansinghka, "Tests of Efficiency Performance of Conglomerate Firms," *Journal of Finance,* September, 1971.

24. The results for tests using equations 2-3 and 2-4 and using rate of return on equity were mixed. U-form firms showed higher elasticity estimates for both the sales and profitability terms. This apparent contradiction with the results using return on assets may be the result of M-form firms being more highly leveraged during the sample period than the U-form firms. This would be an expected result if M-form firms were more expansion minded. That M-form firms were more highly leveraged is presently conjecture. The results using return on equity showed M-form firms penalizing staff expansion bias more heavily than U-form firms for the REMUN and TREM definitions. This differential was not seen for the COMPN and CMPN definitions.

25. Lewellen and Huntsman, "Managerial Pay and Corporate Performance."

Chapter 3

1. Williamson, "Managerial Discretion, Organization Form, and the Multi-Division Hypothesis," p. 367.

2. Ibid.

3. J. Fred Weston and Surenda K. Mansinghka, "Tests of Efficiency Performance of Conglomerate Firms," *Journal of Finance,* 26: 919-936, September, 1971.

4. Ibid., p. 934.

5. Williamson, *Markets and Hierarchies* chapters 8 and 9.

6. This is the type of situation which faced both DuPont and General Motors before they adopted their M-form organization. See: Chandler, *Strategy & Structure.*

7. See appendix D for a list of these firms.

8. An example may be an increase in executive compensation.

9. A check was made on the sensitivity of the results to changes in the length of lag used. The results are similar whether no lag is used or whether a lag of one through five years is used.

10. Even these data are rather aggregated.

11. For a more complete explanation, see: J. Fred Weston, Keith B. Smith, and Ronald E. Shrieves, "Conglomerate Performance Using the Capital Asset Pricing Model," *Review of Economics and Statistics,* 54: 357-363, November, 1972.

12. Chandler, *Strategy and Structure,* p. 369.

13. Ibid.

14. T. Crawford Honeycutt and Donald Zimmerman, "The Measurement of Corporate Diversification: 1950-1957," *The Antitrust Bulletin,* 21: 509-535, Fall, 1976. This study has many problems. Its conclusions should be accepted only with extreme caution. The rank correlations appear to have been performed properly.

15. The debt-equity ratio is not introduced as an independent variable in the CAPM model. Because its effect should be shown by the β term, financial structure does not have an independent effect on rate of return.

16. Hall and Weiss, "Firm Size and Profitability," *Review of Economics and Statistics,* August, 1967, p. 321.

17. Franco Modigliani and Merton H. Miller, "The Cost of Capital, Corporation Finance and the Theory of Investment," *American Economic Review,* 48: 261-297, June, 1958.

18. Twenty-six firms form the sample whenever diversification is included as a variable. This is due to the dropping of Texas Instruments because of insufficient data.

19. Chandler, *Strategy and Structure,* p. 369.

20. Of course the pattern may have occurred randomly. In general, it is a dangerous procedure to draw conclusions from a statistical pattern which is not predicted previous to the testing.

Chapter 4

1. Kaiser Aluminum and Chemical Corporation, *1957 Annual Report.*

2. See: (1) Oliver E. Williamson, "Vertical Integration of Production: Market Failure Considerations," *American Economic Review,* May, 1971. (2) David Teece, *Vertical Integration and Vertical Divestiture in the U.S. Oil Industry,* Stanford University Institute for Energy Studies, (Stanford, California: 1976).

3. The Metals Division was exclusively a production unit. Primary aluminum is not sold in large quantities compared to aluminum fabrications. Sales are usually in relatively large lots and are made to a relatively stable group of buyers.

4. Timothy F. Preece (Vice President, Planning and Administrative Systems, Kaiser Aluminum and Chemical Corporation), letter to author, April 26, 1974.

5. R. Burt Gookin, December 6, 1966.

6. *Management Planning and Control: The J.H. Heinz Approach,* Controllership Foundation, Inc., Controllers Institute of America, 1957.

7. E.J. Mack (Senior Vice President, Burlington Industries), letter to author, March 20, 1974.

8. *Thirty Years of the Burlington Story,* company publication, 1953.

9. Burlington Industries, Inc., *1954 Annual Report.*

10.   Burlington Industries, Inc., *1969 Annual Report.*

11.   T.M. Liptak (Office of the Director of Organization Planning, IBM), letter to author, July 8, 1974.

12.   "Can IBM Keep Up the Pace," *Business Week,* February 2, 1963, p. 93.

13.   Ibid.

14.   T.M. Liptak (Office of the Director of Organization Planning, IBM), letter to author, July 8, 1974.

15.   Paul R. Elsen (Director, Human Resources, Honeywell, Inc.), letter to author, April 19, 1974.

16.   Ibid.

Chapter 5

1.   Williamson, *Markets and Hierarchies,* p. 150.

Appendix A

1.   Lewellen, *The Ownership Income of Management,* p. 20.

2.   Lewellen has conducted sensitivity analysis on executive compensation data and has found that the results are not very sensitive to the choice of interest rate.

Bibliography

Alchian, Armen A., and Harold Demsetz, "Production, Information Costs, and Economic Organization, *American Economic Review*, 62: 777-795, December, 1972.

Armour, Henry Ogden, and David J. Teece, "Organizational Structure and Economic Performance: A Test of the Multidivisional Hypothesis," Draft, August, 1977.

Arrow, Kenneth J., *The Limits of Organization*, New York: W.W. Norton & Company, 1974.

Bain, Joe S., *Barriers to New Competition*, Cambridge, Massachusetts: Harvard University Press, 1956.

Baumol, William, *Behavior, Value, and Growth*, New York: Macmillan, New York, 1959.

Baumol, William J., Peggy Heim, Burton G. Malkiel, and Richard E. Quent, "Earnings Retention, New Capital and the Growth of the Firm," *Review of Economics and Statistics*, 52: 345-355, November, 1970.

Baumol, William J., and Tibor Fabian, "Decomposition Pricing for Decentralization and External Economies," *Management Science*, 11: 1-32, September, 1964.

Berle, Adolf A., and Gardiner C. Means, *The Modern Corporation and Private Property*, Revised Edition, New York: Harcourt, Brace, & World, Inc., 1968.

Bernard, Chester, *The Functions of the Executive*, Cambridge, Massachusetts: Harvard University Press, 1938.

Berry, Charles H., *Corporate Growth and Diversification*, 1975.

Boudreaux, Kenneth J., "'Managerialism' and Risk-Return Performance," *Southern Economic Journal*, 39: 366-372, January, 1973.

Bower, Joseph L., "Planning Within the Firm," *American Economic Review*, 60: 186-194, May, 1970.

Brozen, Yale, "Concentration and Profits: Does Concentration Matter?" *The Antitrust Bulletin*, 19: 381-400, Summer, 1974.

Burlington Industries, Inc., *1954 Annual Report*.

Burlington Industries, Inc., *1969 Annual Report*.

Burlington Industries, Inc., *Thirty Years of the Burlington Story*, 1953.

"Can IBM Keep Up the Pace," *Business Week*, February 2, 1963, p. 93.

Caswell, W. Cameron, "Taking Stock of Divisionalization," *Journal of Business*, 29: 160-171, July, 1956.

Chandler, Alfred D., Jr., *Strategy and Structure: Chapters in the History of the American Industrial Enterprise*, Cambridge, Massachusetts: The MIT Press, 1962.

Chow, Gregory, "Tests of Equality Between Sets of Coefficients in Two Linear Regressions," *Econometrica*, 28: 591-605, July, 1960.

Collins, Norman R., and Lee E. Preston, "Concentration and Price-Cost Margins in Food Manufacturing Industries," *Journal of Industrial Economics*, 14: 226-242, June, 1966.

Controlers Institute of America, *Management Planning and Control: The J.H. Heinz Approach*, Controllership Foundation, Inc., 1957.

Dhrymes, Phoebus, and Mordecai Katz, "Investment, Dividend, and External Finance Behavior of Firms," in *Determinants of Investment Behavior*, NBER Conference, pp. 427-67.

Downs, Anthony, *Inside Bureaucracy*, Boston: Little, Brown and Company, 1966.

Dun & Bradstreet's Million Dollar Directory, Dun & Bradstreet's, Inc., New York: various years.

Economic Report on the Influence of Market Structure on the Profit Performance of Food Manufacturing Firms, Report to the Federal Trade Commission, September, 1969.

Eisner, Robert, and Robert H. Strutz, "Determinants of Business Investment," *Research Study Two*, Commission on Money and Credit, 1960.

Elsen, Paul R., (Director, Human Resources, Honeywell, Inc.), letter to author, April 19, 1974.

Fortune, list of 500 largest U.S. Industrial Corporations, 1972.

Gale, Bradley T., "Market Share and Rate of Return," *Review of Economics and Statistics*, 54: 412-423, November, 1972.

Gookin, R. Burt, December 6, 1966.

Gordon, Robert Aaron, *Business Leadership in the Large Corporation*, Berkeley: University of California Press, 1961.

Grabowski, Henry G., and Dennis C. Mueller, "Managerial and Stockholder Welfare Models of Firm Expenditure," *Review of Economics and Statistics*, 54: 9-37, February, 1972.

Griffin, James M., "Determinants of Price-Cost Margins: Results from a Pooled Sample," Draft, 1965.

Groves, Theodore, "Incentives in Teams," *Econometrica*, 41: 617-632, July, 1973.

Hall, M., and L.W. Weiss, "Firm Size and Profitability," *Review of Economics and Statistics*, 49: 319-331, August, 1967.

Heal, G.M., *The Theory of Economic Planning*, New York: American Elsevier Publishing Company, 1973.

Hirschman, Albert O., *Exit, Voice, and Loyalty: Responses to Declines in Firms, Organizations, and States*, Cambridge, Massachusetts: Harvard University Press, 1970.

Hirshleifer, Jack, "On the Economics of Transfer Pricing," *Journal of Business*, 29: 172-184, July, 1956.

Honeycutt, T. Crawford, and Donald Zimmerman, "The Measurement of Corporate Diversification: 1950-1967," *The Antitrust Bulletin*, 21: 509-535, Fall, 1976.

Hurdle, Gloria J., "Leverage, Risk, Market Structure and Profitability," *Review of Economics and Statistics*, 56: 478-485, November, 1974.

Hurwicz, Leonid, "On Informationally Decentralized Systems," in *Decision and Organization*, C.B. McGuire and Roy Radner, eds., Amsterdam: North-Holland, 1972, pp. 297-336.

Johnson, J., *Econometrica Methods*, 2nd Edition, New York: McGraw-Hill Book Company, 1972.

Kaiser Aluminum and Chemical Corporation, *1957 Annual Report*.

Kamerschen, David R., "The Influence of Ownership and Control on Profit Rates," *American Economic Review*, 58: 432-447, June, 1968.

Larner, Robert J., *Management Control and the Large Corporation*, New York: Dunellen Publishing Company, 1970.

Leibenstein, Harvey, "Allocative Efficiency vs. X-Efficiency," *American Economic Review*, 56: 392-415, June, 1966.

Lewellen, Wilbur G., *The Ownership Income of Management*, National Bureau of Economic Research—Fiscal Studies 14, New York, 1971.

Lewellen, Wilbur G., and Blaine Huntsman, "Managerial Pay and Corporate Performance," *American Economic Review*, 60: 710-720, September, 1970.

Lintner, John, "Distribution of Income of Corporations Among Dividends, Retained Earnings and Taxes," *American Economic Review*, 46: 97-113, May, 1956.

Liptak, T.M., (Office of the Director of Organization Planning, IBM), letter to author, July 8, 1974.

Litzenberger, Robert H., and O. Maurice Joy, "Decentralized Capital Budgeting Decisions and Shareholder Wealth Maximization," *Journal of Finance,* 30: 993-1002, September, 1975.

Mack, E.J., (Senior Vice President, Burlington Industries, Inc.). letter to author, March 20, 1974.

Mann, H. Michael, "Seller Concentration, Barriers to Entry, and Rates of Return in Thirty Industries, 1950-1960," *Review of Economics and Statistics,* 48: 296-307, August, 1966.

Marris, Robin, "A Model of the 'Managerial' Enterprise," *Quarterly Journal of Economics,* 77: 185-209, May, 1963.

_____, *The Economic Theory of 'Managerial' Capitalism,* London: Macmillan, 1966.

Masson, Robert, "Executive Motivations, Earnings, and Consequent Equity Performance," *Journal of Political Economy,* 79: 1278-1292, November/December 1971.

McGuire, Joseph W., John S.Y. Chiu, and Alvar O. Elbing, "Executive Incomes, Sales, and Profits," *American Economic Review,* 52: 753-761, September, 1962.

Modigliani, Franco, and Merton H. Miller, "The Cost of Capital, Corporation Finance and the Theory of Investment," *American Economic Review,* 48: 261-297, June, 1958.

Monsen, R. Joseph, and Anthony Downs, "A Theory of Large Managerial Firms," *Journal of Political Economy,* 73: 221-236, June, 1965.

Moody's Industrial Manual, Moody's Investor Service, Inc., New York: various years.

Mueller, Dennis C., "A Theory of Conglomerate Mergers," *Quarterly Journal of Economics,* 83: 643-659, 1969.

Nerlove, Marc, *Estimation and Identification of Cobb-Douglas Production Functions.*

_____, "Factors Affecting Differences Among Rates of Return on Investments in Individual Common Stocks," *Review of Economics and Statistics,* 1968.

Olson, Mancur, *The Logic of Collective Action,* Revised Edition, New York: Schocken Books, 1971.

Palmer, John, "The Profit-Performance Effects of the Separation of Ownership from Control in Large U.S. Industrial Corporations," *The Bell Journal of Economics and Management Science,* 5: 293-303, Spring, 1973.

Preece, Timothy F., (Vice President, Planning and Administrative Systems, Kaiser Aluminum and Chemical Corporation), letter to author, April 26, 1974.

Roberts, David R., *Executive Compensation,* Glencoe, Illinois: The Free Press, 1959.

Schelling, Thomas C., *The Strategy of Conflict,* New York: Oxford University Press, 1960.

Scherer, F.M., *Industrial Market Structure and Economic Performance,* Chicago: Rand McNally & Company, 1971.

Sharpe, William F., "Capital Asset Prices: A Theory of Market Equilibrium Under Conditions of Risk," *The Journal of Finance,* 19: 425-442, September, 1964.

Shepherd, William G., "The Elements of Market Structure," *Review of Economics and Statistics,* 54: 25-37, February, 1972.

Simon, Herbert, *Administrative Behavior,* Second Edition, New York: The Free Press, 1957.

_____, "The Compensation of Executives," *Sociometry,* March, 1957, pp. 32-35.

_____, "Theories of Bounded Rationality," in *Decision and Organization,* C.B. McGuire and Roy Rander, eds., Amsterdam: North-Holland, 1972, pp. 161-76.

Standard & Poor's COMPUSTAT Data Service.

Standard & Poor's Industry Studies.

Teece, David, *Vertical Integration and Vertical Divestiture in the U.S. Oil Industry,* Stanford University Institute for Energy Studies, Stanford, California, 1976.

Thompson, James D., *Organizations in Action,* New York: McGraw-Hill Book Company, 1967.

Vernon, John M., *Market Structure and Industrial Performance: A Review of Statistical Findings,* Boston: Allyn and Bacon, Inc., 1972.

Weiss, Leonard W., "The Concentration-Profits Relationship and Antitrust," in *Industrial Concentration: The New Learning,* Harvey J. Goldschmid, H. Michael Mann, and J. Fred Weston, eds., Boston: Little, Brown and Company, 1974.

Weston, J. Fred, and Surenda Mansinghka, "Tests of Efficiency Performance of Conglomerate Firms," *Journal of Finance,* 26: 919-936, September, 1971.

Weston, J. Fred, Keith B. Smith, and Ronald E. Shrieves, "Conglomerate Performance Using the Capital Asset Pricing Model," *Review of Economics and Statistics,* 54: 357-363, November, 1972.

Williamson, Oliver E., and Narotum Bhargava, "Assessing and Classifying the Internal Structure and Control Apparatus of the Modern Corporation," in: *Market Structure and Corporate Behavior: Theory and Empirical Analysis of the Firm,* Keith Cowling, ed., London: Gray-Mills Publishing Ltd., 1972, pp. 125-48.

Williamson, Oliver E., *Corporate Control and Business Behavior,* Englewood Cliffs, New Jersey: Prentice Hall, Inc., 1970.

———, *The Economics of Discretionary Behavior: Managerial Objectives in a Theory of the Firm,* Englewood Cliffs, New Jersey: Prentice-Hall, Inc., 1964.

———, "Managerial Discretion, Organization Form, and the Multi-Division Hypothesis," in: *The Corporate Economy,* Robin Marris and Adrian Wood, ed., 1971, pp. 343-86.

———, *Markets and Hierarchies: Analysis and Antitrust Considerations,* New York: The Free Press, 1975.

———, "Vertical Integration of Production: Market Failure Considerations," *American Economic Review,* May, 1971.

Wrigley, Leonard, "Divisional Autonomy and Diversification," Ph.D. dissertation, Harvard University Business School, 1970.

Yarrow, in *Market Structure and Corporate Behavior: Theory and Empirical Analysis of the Firm,* Keith Cowling, ed., London: Gray-Mills Publishing Ltd., 1972.

Index